# All Things
# Bright and Beautiful

Also Available in Large Print
by James Herriot

*All Creatures Great and Small*

# All Things Bright and Beautiful

## JAMES HERRIOT

## VOL. I

G.K.HALL&CO.

 Boston, Massachusetts

1975

Library of Congress Cataloging in Publication Data

Herriot, James.
   All things bright and beautiful.

   "Published in large print."
   1. Herriot, James.  2. Veterinarians—Correspondence, reminis-
cences, etc.   3. Sight-saving books.
I.  Title.
[SF613.H44A283 1975]      636.089′092′4 [B]
ISBN 0-8161-6269-7                                          74-32391

Published in Large Print by arrangement with St. Martin's Press

Set in Photon 18 pt Crown

With love
to
MY WIFE
and to
MY MOTHER
In dear old Glasgow town

All things bright and beautiful,
    All creatures great and small,
All things wise and wonderful,
    The Lord God made them all.
                *Cecil Francis Alexander*
                        *1818-1895*

# Chapter 1

As I crawled into bed and put my arm around Helen it occurred to me, not for the first time, that there are few pleasures in this world to compare with snuggling up to a nice woman when you are half frozen.

There weren't any electric blankets in the thirties. Which was a pity because nobody needed the things more than country vets. It is surprising how deeply bone-marrow cold a man can get when he is dragged from his bed in the small hours and made to strip off in farm buildings when his metabolism is at a low ebb. Often the worst part was coming back to bed; I often lay exhausted for over an hour, longing for sleep but kept awake until my icy limbs and feet had thawed out.

But since my marriage such things were but a dark memory. Helen stirred in her sleep — she had got used to her husband leaving her in the night and returning like a blast from the North Pole — and instinctively moved nearer to me. With a sigh of thankfulness I felt the blissful warmth envelop me and almost immediately the events of the last two hours began to recede into unreality.

It had started with the aggressive shrilling of the bedside phone at one a.m. And it was Sunday morning, a not unusual time for some farmers after a late Saturday night to have a look round their stock and decide to send for the vet.

This time it was Harold Ingledew. And it struck me right away that he would have just about had time to get back to his farm after his ten pints at the Four Horse Shoes where they weren't too fussy about closing time.

And there was a significant slurr in the thin croak of his voice.

'I 'ave a ewe amiss. Will you come?'

'Is she very bad?' In my semi-conscious state I always clung to the faint hope that one night somebody would say it would wait till morning. It had never happened yet and it didn't happen now: Mr Ingledew was not to be denied.

'Aye, she's in a bad way. She'll have to have summat done for 'er soon.'

Not a minute to lose, I thought bitterly. But she had probably been in a bad way all the evening when Harold was out carousing.

Still, there were compensations. A sick sheep didn't present any great threat. It was worst when you have to get out of bed facing the prospect of a spell of sheer hard labour in your enfeebled state. But in this case I was confident that I would be able to adopt my half-awake technique; which meant simply that I would be able to go out there and deal with the emergency and return between the sheets while still enjoying many of the benefits of sleep.

There was so much night work in country practice that I had been compelled to perfect this system as, I suspect, had many of my fellow practitioners. I had done some sterling work while in a somnambulistic limbo.

So, eyes closed, I tiptoed across the

carpet and pulled on my working clothes. I effortlessly accomplished the journey down the long flights of stairs but when I opened the side door the system began to crumble, because even in the shelter of the high-walled garden the wind struck at me with savage force. It was difficult to stay asleep. In the yard as I backed out of the garage the high branches of the elms groaned in the darkness as they bent before the blast.

Driving from the town I managed to slip back into my trance and my mind played lazily with the phenomenon of Harold Ingledew. This drinking of his was so out of character. He was a tiny mouse of a man about seventy years old and when he came into the surgery on an occasional market day it was difficult to extract more than a few muttered words from him. Dressed in his best suit, his scrawny neck protruding from a shirt collar several sizes too big for him, he was the very picture of a meek and solid citizen; the watery blue eyes and fleshless cheeks added to the effect and only the brilliant red colouration of the tip of his nose gave

4

any hint of other possibilities.

His fellow smallholders in Therby village were all steady characters and did not indulge beyond a social glass of beer now and then, and his next door neighbour had been somewhat bitter when he spoke to me a few weeks ago.

'He's nowt but a bloody nuisance is awd Harold.'

'How do you mean?'

'Well, every Saturday night and every market night he's up roarin' and singin' till four o'clock in the mornin'.'

'Harold Ingledew? Surely not! He's such a quiet little chap.'

'Aye, he is for the rest of t'week.'

'But I can't imagine him singing!'

'You should live next door to 'im, Mr Herriot. He makes a 'ell of a racket. There's no sleep for anybody till he settles down.'

Since then I had heard from another source that this was perfectly true and that Mrs Ingledew tolerated it because her husband was entirely submissive at all other times.

The road to Therby had a few sharp

little switchbacks before it dipped to the village and looking down I could see the long row of silent houses curving away to the base of the fell which by day hung in peaceful green majesty over the huddle of roofs but now bulked black and menacing under the moon.

As I stepped from the car and hurried round to the back of the house the wind caught at me again, jerking me to wakefulness as though somebody had thrown a bucket of water over me. But for a moment I forgot the cold in the feeling of shock as the noise struck me. Singing . . . loud raucous singing echoing around the old stones of the yard.

It was coming from the lighted kitchen window.

'JUST A SONG AT TWILIGHT, WHEN THE LIGHTS ARE LOW!'

I looked inside and saw little Harold sitting with his stockinged feet extended towards the dying embers of the fire while one hand clutched a bottle of brown ale.

'AND THE FLICKERING SHADOWS SOFTLY COME AND GO!' He was really letting it rip, head back, mouth wide.

I thumped on the kitchen door.

'THOUGH THE HEART BE WEARY, SAD THE DAY AND LONG!' replied Harold's reedy tenor and I banged impatiently at the woodwork again.

The noise ceased and I waited an unbelievably long time till I heard the key turning and the bolt rattling back. The little man pushed his nose out and gave me a questioning look.

'I've come to see your sheep,' I said.

'Oh aye.' He nodded curtly with none of his usual diffidence. 'Ah'll put me boots on.' He banged the door in my face and I heard the bolt shooting home.

Taken aback as I was I realised that he wasn't being deliberately rude. Bolting the door was proof that he was doing everything mechanically. But for all that he had left me standing in an uncharitable spot. Vets will tell you that there are corners in farm yards which are colder than any hill top and I was in one now. Just beyond the kitchen door was a stone archway leading to the open fields and through this black opening there whistled a Siberian draught which cut effortlessly

7

through my clothes.

I had begun to hop from one foot to the other when the singing started again.

'THERE'S AN OLD MILL BY THE STREAM, NELLIE DEAN!'

Horrified, I rushed back to the window. Harold was back in his chair, pulling on a vast boot and taking his time about it. As he bellowed he poked owlishly at the lace holes and occasionally refreshed himself from the bottle of brown ale.

I tapped on the window. 'Please hurry, Mr Ingledew.'

'WHERE WE USED TO SIT AND DREAM, NELLIE DEAN!' bawled Harold in response.

My teeth had begun to chatter before he got both boots on but at last he reappeared in the doorway.

'Come on then,' I gasped. 'Where is this ewe? Have you got her in one of these boxes?'

The old man raised his eyebrows. 'Oh, she's not 'ere.'

'Not here?'

'Nay, she's up at t'top buildings.'

'Right back up the road, you mean?'

'Aye, ah stopped off on t'way home and had a look at 'er.'

I stamped and rubbed my hands. 'Well, we'll have to drive back up. But there's no water, is there? You'd better bring a bucket of warm water, some soap and a towel.'

'Very good.' He nodded solemnly and before I knew what was happening the door was slammed shut and bolted and I was alone again in the darkness. I trotted immediately to the window and was not surprised to see Harold seated comfortably again. He leaned forward and lifted the kettle from the hearth and for a dreadful moment I thought he was going to start heating the water on the ashes of the fire. But with a gush of relief I saw him take hold of a ladle and reach into the primitive boiler in the old black grate.

'AND THE WATERS AS THEY FLOW SEEM TO MURMUR SWEET AND LOW!' he warbled, happy at his work, as he unhurriedly filled a bucket.

I think he had forgotten I was there when he finally came out because he

9

looked at me blankly as he sang.

'YOU'RE MY HEART'S DESIRE, I LOVE YOU, NELLIE DEAN!' he informed me at the top of his voice.

'All right, all right,' I grunted. 'Let's go.' I hurried him into the car and we set off on the way I had come.

Harold held the bucket at an angle on his lap, and as we went over the switchbacks the water slopped gently on to my knee. The atmosphere in the car soon became so highly charged with beer fumes that I began to feel light headed.

'In 'ere!' the old man barked suddenly as a gate appeared in the headlights. I pulled on to the grass verge and stood on one leg for a few moments till I had shaken a surplus pint or two of water from my trousers. We went through the gate and I began to hurry towards the dark bulk of the hillside barn, but I noticed that Harold wasn't following me. He was walking aimlessly around the field.

'What are you doing, Mr Ingledew?'

'Lookin' for t'ewe.'

'You mean she's outside?' I repressed an impulse to scream.

'Aye, she lambed this afternoon and ah thowt she'd be right enough out 'ere.' He produced a torch, a typical farmer's torch — tiny and with a moribund battery — and projected a fitful beam into the darkness. It made not the slightest difference.

As I stumbled across the field a sense of hopelessness assailed me. Above, the ragged clouds scurried across the face of the moon but down here I could see nothing. And it was so cold. The recent frosts had turned the ground to iron and the crisp grass cowered under the piercing wind. I had just decided that there was no way of finding an animal in this black waste land when Harold piped up.

'She's over 'ere.'

And sure enough when I groped my way towards the sound of his voice he was standing by an unhappy looking ewe. I don't know what instinct had brought him to her but there she was. And she was obviously in trouble; her head hung down miserably and when I put my hand on her fleece she took only a few faltering steps

11

instead of galloping off as a healthy sheep would. Beside her, a tiny lamb huddled close to her flank.

I lifted her tail and took her temperature. It was normal. There were no signs of the usual post-lambing ailments; no staggering to indicate a deficiency, no discharge or accelerated respirations. But there was something very far wrong.

I looked again at the lamb. He was an unusually early arrival in this high country and it seemed unfair to bring the little creature into the inhospitable world of a Yorkshire March. And he was so small . . . yes . . . yes . . . it was beginning to filter through to me. He was too damn small for a single lamb.

'Bring me that bucket, Mr Ingledew!' I cried. I could hardly wait to see if I was right. But as I balanced the receptacle on the grass the full horror of the situation smote me. I was going to have to strip off.

They don't give vets medals for bravery but as I pulled off my overcoat and jacket and stood shivering in my shirt sleeves on that black hillside I felt I deserved one.

'Hold her head,' I gasped and soaped my arm quickly. By the light of the torch I felt my way into the vagina and I didn't have to go very far before I found what I expected; a woolly little skull. It was bent downwards with the nose under the pelvis and the legs were back.

'There's another lamb in here,' I said. 'It's laid wrong or it would have been born with its mate this afternoon.'

Even as I spoke my fingers had righted the presentation and I drew the little creature gently out and deposited him on the grass. I hadn't expected him to be alive after his delayed entry but as he made contact with the cold ground his limbs gave a convulsive twitch and almost immediately I felt his ribs heaving under my hand.

For a moment I forgot the knife-like wind in the thrill which I always found in new life, the thrill that was always fresh, always warm. The ewe, too, seemed stimulated because in the darkness I felt her nose pushing interestedly at the new arrival.

But my pleasant ruminations were cut

short by a scuffling from behind me and some muffled words.

'Bugger it!' mumbled Harold.

'What's the matter?'

'Ah've kicked bucket ower.'

'Oh no! Is the water all gone?'

'Aye, nowt left.'

Well this was great. My arm was smeared with mucus after being inside the ewe. I couldn't possibly put my jacket on without a wash.

Harold's voice issued again from the darkness. 'There's some watter ower at building.'

'Oh good. We've got to get this ewe and lambs over there anyway.' I threw my clothes over my shoulder, tucked a lamb under each arm and began to blunder over the tussocks of grass to where I thought the barn lay. The ewe, clearly feeling better without her uncomfortable burden, trotted behind me.

It was Harold again who had to give me directions.

'Ower 'ere!' he shouted.

When I reached the barn I cowered thankfully behind the massive stones. It was no night for a stroll in shirt sleeves. Shaking uncontrollably I peered at the old man. I could just see his form in the last faint radiance of the torch and I wasn't quite sure what he was doing. He had lifted a stone from the pasture and was bashing something with it; then I realised he was bending over the water trough, breaking the ice.

When he had finished he plunged the bucket into the trough and handed it to me.

'There's your watter,' he said triumphantly.

I thought I had reached the ultimate in frigidity but when I plunged my hands into the black liquid with its floating icebergs I changed my mind. The torch had finally expired and I lost the soap very quickly. When I found I was trying to work up a lather with one of the pieces of ice I gave it up and dried my arms.

Somewhere nearby I could hear Harold humming under his breath, as comfortable as if he was by his own fireside. The vast amount of alcohol surging through his blood stream must have made him impervious to the cold.

We pushed the ewe and lambs into the barn which was piled high with hay and before leaving I struck a match and looked down at the little sheep and her new family settled comfortably among the fragrant clover. They would be safe and warm in there till morning.

My journey back to the village was less hazardous because the bucket on Harold's knee was empty. I dropped him outside his house then I had to drive to the bottom of the village to turn; and as I came past the house again the sound forced its way into the car.

'IF YOU WERE THE ONLY GIRL IN THE WORLD AND I WERE THE ONLY BOY!'

I stopped, wound the window down and listened in wonder. It was incredible how the noise reverberated around the quiet street and if it went on till four o'clock in the morning as the neighbours said, then they had my sympathy.

'NOTHING ELSE WOULD MATTER IN THE WORLD TODAY!'

It struck me suddenly that I could soon

get tired of Harold's singing. His volume was impressive but for all that he would never be in great demand at Covent Garden; he constantly wavered off key and there was a grating quality in his top notes which set my teeth on edge.

'WE WOULD GO ON LOVING IN THE SAME OLD WAY!'

Hurriedly I wound the window up and drove off. As the heaterless car picked its way between the endless flitting pattern of walls I crouched in frozen immobility behind the wheel. I had now reached the state of total numbness and I can't remember much about my return to the yard at Skeldale House, nor my automatic actions of putting away the car, swinging shut the creaking doors of what had once been the old coach house, and trailing slowly down the long garden.

But a realisation of my blessings began to return when I slid into bed and Helen, instead of shrinking away from me as it would have been natural to do, deliberately draped her feet and legs over the human ice block that was her husband. The bliss was unbelievable. It was worth getting out just to come back to this.

I glanced at the luminous dial of the alarm clock. It was three o'clock and as the warmth flowed over me and I drifted away, my mind went back to the ewe and lambs, snug in their scented barn. They would be asleep now, I would soon be asleep, everybody would be asleep.

Except, that is, Harold Ingledew's neighbours. They still had an hour to go.

# Chapter 2

I had only to sit up in bed to look right across Darrowby to the hills beyond.

I got up and walked to the window. It was going to be a fine morning and the early sun glanced over the weathered reds and greys of the jumbled roofs, some of them sagging under their burden of ancient tiles, and brightened the tufts of green where trees pushed upwards from the gardens among the bristle of chimney pots. And behind everything the calm bulk of the fells.

It was my good fortune that this was the first thing I saw every morning; after Helen, of course, which was better still.

Following our unorthodox tuberculin testing honeymoon we had set up our first home on the top of Skeldale House. Siegfried, my boss up to my wedding and now my partner, had offered us free use of these empty rooms on the third storey and we had gratefully accepted; and though it was a makeshift arrangement there was an airy charm, an exhilaration in our high perch that many would have envied.

It was makeshift because everything at that time had a temporary complexion and we had no idea how long we would be there. Siegfried and I had both volunteered for the R.A.F and were on deferred service but that is all I am going to say about the war. This book is not about such things which in any case were so very far from Darrowby; it is the story of the months I had with Helen between our marriage and my call-up and is about the ordinary things which have always made up our lives; my work, the animals, the Dales.

This front room was our bed-sitter and though it was not luxuriously furnished it did have an excellent bed, a carpet, a handsome side table which had belonged to Helen's mother and two armchairs. It had an ancient wardrobe, too, but the lock didn't work and the only way we kept the door closed was by jamming one of my socks in it. The toe always dangled outside but it never seemed of any importance.

I went out and across a few feet of landing to our kitchen-dining room at the back. This apartment was definitely spartan. I clumped over bare boards to a bench we had rigged against the wall by the window. This held a gas ring and our crockery and cutlery. I seized a tall jug and began my long descent to the main kitchen downstairs because one minor snag was that there was no water at the top of the house. Down two flights to the three rooms on the first storey then down two more and a final gallop along the passage to the big stone-flagged kitchen at the end.

I filled the jug and returned to our eyrie two steps at a time. I wouldn't like to do this now whenever I needed water but at that time I didn't find it the least inconvenience.

Helen soon had the kettle boiling and we drank our first cup of tea by the window looking down on the long garden. From up here we had an aerial view of the unkempt lawns, the fruit trees, the wisteria climbing the weathered brick towards our window, and the high walls with their old stone copings stretching away to the cobbled yard under the elms. Every day I went up and down that path to the garage in the yard but it looked so different from above.

'Wait a minute, Helen,' I said. 'Let me sit on that chair.'

She had laid the breakfast on the bench where we ate and this was where the difficulty arose. Because it was a tall bench and our recently acquired high stool fitted it but our chair didn't.

'No, I'm all right, Jim, really I am.' She smiled at me reassuringly from her absurd position, almost at eye level with her plate.

'You can't be all right,' I retorted. 'Your chin's nearly in among your corn flakes. Please let me sit there.'

She patted the seat of the stool. 'Come on, stop arguing. Sit down and have your breakfast.'

This, I felt, just wouldn't do. I tried a different tack.

'Helen!' I said severely. 'Get off that chair!'

'No!' she replied without looking at me, her lips pushed forward in a characteristic pout which I always found enchanting but which also meant she wasn't kidding.

I was at a loss. I toyed with the idea of pulling her off the chair, but she was a big girl. We had had a previous physical try-out when a minor disagreement had escalated into a wrestling match and though I thoroughly enjoyed the contest and actually won in the end I had been surprised by her sheer strength. At this time in the morning I didn't feel up to it. I sat on the stool.

After breakfast Helen began to boil water for the washing-up, the next stage in our routine. Meanwhile I went downstairs, collected my gear, including suture material for a foal which had cut its leg and went out the side door into the garden. Just about opposite the rockery I turned and looked up at our window. It was open at the bottom and an arm emerged holding a dishcloth. I waved and the dishcloth waved back furiously. It was the start to every day.

And, driving from the yard, it seemed a good start. In fact everything was good. The raucous cawing of the rooks in the elms above as I closed the double doors, the clean fragrance of the air which greeted me every morning, and the challenge and interest of my job.

The injured foal was at Robert Corner's farm and I hadn't been there long before I spotted Jock, his sheep dog. And I began to watch the dog because behind a vet's daily chore of treating his patients there is always the fascinating kaleidoscope of animal personality and Jock was an interesting case.

A lot of farm dogs are partial to a little light relief from their work. They like to play and one of their favourite games is chasing cars off the premises. Often I drove off with a hairy form galloping alongside and the dog would usually give a final defiant bark after a few hundred yards to speed me on my way. But Jock was different.

He was really dedicated. Car chasing to

him was a deadly serious art which he practised daily without a trace of levity. Corner's farm was at the end of a long track, twisting for nearly a mile between its stone walls down through the gently sloping fields to the road below and Jock didn't consider he had done his job properly until he had escorted his chosen vehicle right to the very foot. So his hobby was an exacting one.

I watched him now as I finished stitching the foal's leg and began to tie on a bandage. He was slinking about the buildings, a skinny little creature who without his mass of black and white hair would have been an almost invisible mite, and he was playing out a transparent charade of pretending he was taking no notice of me — wasn't the least bit interested in my presence, in fact. But his furtive glances in the direction of the stable, his repeated criss-crossing of my line of vision gave him away. He was waiting for his big moment.

When I was putting on my shoes and throwing my wellingtons into the boot I saw him again. Or rather part of him;

just a long nose and one eye protruding from beneath a broken door. It wasn't till I had started the engine and begun to move off that he finally declared himself, stealing out from his hiding place, body low, tail trailing, eyes fixed intently on the car's front wheels, and as I gathered speed and headed down the track he broke into an effortless lope.

I had been through this before and was always afraid he might run in front of me so I put my foot down and began to hurtle downhill. This was where Jock came into his own. I often wondered how he'd fare against a racing greyhound because by golly he could run. That sparse frame housed a perfect physical machine and slender limbs reached and flew again and again, devouring the stony ground beneath, keeping up with the speeding car with joyful ease.

There was a sharp bend about half way down and here Jock invariably sailed over the wall and streaked across the turf, a little dark blur against the green, and having craftily cut off the corner he reappeared like a missile zooming over the grey stones lower down. This put him into a nice position for the run to the road and when he finally saw me on to the tarmac my last view of him was of a happy, panting face looking after me. Clearly he considered it was a job well done and he would wander contentedly back up to the farm to await the next session, perhaps with the postman or the baker's van.

And there was another side to Jock. He was an outstanding performer at the sheepdog trials and Mr Corner had won many trophies with him. In fact the farmer could have sold the little animal for a lot of money but couldn't be persuaded to part with him. Instead he purchased a bitch, a scrawny little female counterpart of Jock and a trial winner in her own right. With this combination Mr Corner thought he could breed some world-beating types for sale. On my visits to the farm the bitch joined in the car-chasing but it seemed as though she was doing it more or less to humour her new mate and she always gave up at the first bend leaving Jock in command. You could see her heart wasn't in it.

When the pups arrived, seven fluffy black balls tumbling about the yard and getting under everybody's feet, Jock watched indulgently as they tried to follow him in his pursuit of my vehicle and you could almost see him laughing as they fell over their feet and were left trailing far behind.

It happened that I didn't have to go there for about ten months but I saw Robert Corner in the market occasionally and he told me he was training the pups and they were shaping well. Not that they needed much training; it was in their blood and he said they had tried to round up the cattle and sheep nearly as soon as they could walk. When I finally saw them they were like seven Jocks — meagre, darting little creatures flitting noiselessly about the buildings — and it didn't take me long to find out that they had learned more than sheep herding from their father. There was something very evocative about the way they began to prowl around in the background as I prepared to get into my car, peeping furtively from behind straw bales, slinking with elaborate nonchalance into favourable positions for a quick getaway. And as I settled in my seat I could sense they were all crouched in readiness for the off.

I revved my engine, let in the clutch with a bump and shot across the yard and in a second the immediate vicinity erupted in a mass of hairy forms. I roared on to the track and put my foot down and on either side of me the little animals pelted along shoulder to shoulder, their faces all wearing the intent fanatical expression I knew so well. When Jock cleared the wall the seven pups went with him and when they reappeared and entered the home straight I noticed something different. On past occasions Jock had always had one eye on the car — this was what he considered his opponent; but now on that last quarter mile as he hurtled along at the head of a shaggy phalanx he was glancing at the pups on either side as though they were the main opposition.

And there was no doubt he was in

trouble. Superbly fit though he was, these stringy bundles of bone and sinew which he had fathered had all his speed plus the newly minted energy of youth and it was taking every shred of his power to keep up with them. Indeed there was one terrible moment when he stumbled and was engulfed by the bounding creatures around him; it seemed that all was lost but there was a core of steel in Jock. Eyes popping, nostrils dilated, he fought his way through the pack until by the time we reached the road he was once more in the lead.

But it had taken its toll. I slowed down before driving away and looked down at the little animal standing with lolling tongue and heaving flanks on the grass verge. It must have been like this with all the other vehicles and it wasn't a merry game any more. I supose it sounds silly to say you could read a dog's thoughts but everything in his posture betrayed the mounting apprehension that his days of supremacy were numbered. Just round the corner lay the unthinkable ignominy of being left trailing in the rear of that litter of young upstarts and as I drew away Jock looked after me and his expression was eloquent.

'How long can I keep this up?'

I felt for the little dog and on my next visit to the farm about two months later I wasn't looking forward to witnessing the final degradation which I felt was inevitable. But when I drove into the yard I found the place strangely unpopulated.

Robert Corner was forking hay into the cow's racks in the byre. He turned as I came in.

'Where are all your dogs?' I asked.

He put down his fork. 'All gone. By gaw, there's a market for good workin' sheep dogs. I've done right well out of t'job.'

'But you've still got Jock?'

'Oh aye, ah couldn't part with t'awd lad. He's over there.'

And so he was, creeping around as of old, pretending he wasn't watching me. And when the happy time finally arrived and I drove away it was like it used to be with the lean little animal haring along by the side of the car, but relaxed, enjoying the game, winging effortlessly over the wall and beating the car down to the tarmac with no trouble at all.

I think I was as relieved as he was that he was left alone with his supremacy unchallenged; that he was still top dog.

# Chapter 3

This was my third spring in the Dales but it was like the two before — and all the springs after. The kind of spring, that is, that a country vet knows; the din of the lambing pens, the bass rumble of the ewes and the high, insistent bawling of the lambs. This, for me, has always heralded the end of winter and the beginning of something new. This and the piercing Yorkshire wind and the hard, bright sunshine flooding the bare hillsides.

At the top of the grassy slope the pens, built of straw bales, formed a long row of square cubicles each holding a ewe with her lambs and I could see Rob Benson coming round the far end carrying two feeding buckets. Rob was hard at it; at this time of the year he didn't go to bed for about six weeks; he would maybe take off his boots and doze by the kitchen fire at night but he was his own shepherd and never very far from the scene of action.

'Ah've got a couple of cases for you today, Jim.' His face, cracked and purpled by the weather, broke into a grin. 'It's not really you ah need, it's that little lady's hand of yours and right sharpish, too.'

He led the way to a bigger enclosure, holding several sheep. There was a scurry as we went in but he caught expertly at the fleece of a darting ewe. 'This is the first one. You can see we haven't a deal o' time.'

I lifted the woolly tail and gasped. The lamb's head was protruding from the vagina, the lips of the vulva clamped tightly behind the ears, and it had swollen enormously to more than twice its size. The eyes were mere puffed slits in the great oedematous ball and the tongue, blue and engorged, lolled from the mouth.

'Well I've seen a few big heads, Rob, but I think this takes the prize.'

Aye, the little beggar came with his legs back. Just beat me to it. Ah was only away for an hour but he was up like a football. By hell it doesn't take long. I know he wants his legs bringin' round but what can I do with bloody great mitts like mine.' He held out his huge hands, rough and swollen with the years of work.

While he spoke I was stripping off my jacket and as I rolled my shirt sleeves high the wind struck like a knife at my shrinking flesh. I soaped my fingers quickly and began to feel for a space round the lamb's neck. For a moment the little eyes opened and regarded me disconsolately.

'He's alive, anyway,' I said. 'But he must feel terrible and he can't do a thing about it.'

Easing my way round, I found a space down by the throat where I thought I might get through. This was where my 'lady's hand' came in useful and I blessed it every spring; I could work inside the ewes with the minimum of discomfort to them and this was all-important because sheep, despite their outdoor hardiness, just won't stand rough treatment.

With the utmost care I inched my way along the curly wool of the neck to the shoulder. Another push forward and I was able to hook a finger round the leg and draw it forward until I could feel the flexure of the knee; a little more twiddling and I had hold of the tiny cloven foot and drew it gently out into the light of day.

Well that was half the job done. I got up from the sack where I was kneeling and went over to the bucket of warm water; I'd use my left hand for the other leg and began to soap it thoroughly while one of the ewes, marshalling her lambs around her, glared at me indignantly and gave a warning stamp of her foot.

Turning, I kneeled again and began the same procedure and as I once more groped forward a tiny lamb dodged under my arm and began to suck at my patient's udder. He was clearly enjoying it, too, if the little tail, twirling inches from my face, meant anything.

'Where did this bloke come from?' I asked, still feeling round.

The farmer smiled. 'Oh that's Herbert. Poor little youth's mother won't have 'im at any price. Took a spite at him at birth though she thinks world of her other lamb.'

'Do you feed him, then?'

'Nay, I was going to put him with the pet lambs but I saw he was fendin' for himself. He pops from one ewe to t'other and gets a quick drink whenever he gets chance. I've never seen owt like it.'

'Only a week old and an independent spirit, eh?'

'That's about the size of it, Jim. I notice 'is belly's full every mornin' so I reckon his ma must let him have a do during the night. She can't see him in the dark — it must be the look of him she can't stand.'

I watched the little creature for a moment. To me he seemed as full of knock-kneed charm as any of the others. Sheep were funny things.

I soon had the other leg out and once that obstruction was removed the lamb followed easily. He was a grotesque sight lying on the strawed grass, his enormous head dwarfing his body, but his ribs were heaving reassuringly and I knew the head would shrink back to normal as quickly as it had expanded. I had another search round inside the ewe but the uterus

37

was empty.

'There's no more, Rob,' I said.

The farmer grunted. 'Aye, I thowt so, just a big single 'un. They're the ones that cause the trouble.'

Drying my arms, I watched Herbert. He had left my patient when she moved round to lick her lamb and he was moving speculatively among the other ewes. Some of them warned him off with a shake of the head but eventually he managed to sneak up on a big, wide-bodied sheep and pushed his head underneath her. Immediately she swung round and with a fierce upward butt of her hard skull she sent the little animal flying high in the air in a whirl of flailing legs. He landed with a thud on his back and as I hurried towards him he leaped to his feet and trotted away.

'Awd bitch!' shouted the farmer and as I turned to him in some concern he shrugged. 'I know, poor little sod, it's rough, but I've got a feelin' he wants it this way rather than being in the pen with the pet lambs. Look at 'im now.'

Herbert, quite unabashed, was

approaching another ewe and as she bent over her feeding trough he nipped underneath her and his tail went into action again. There was no doubt about it — that lamb had guts.

'Rob,' I said as he caught my second patient. 'Why do you call him Herbert?'

'Well that's my youngest lad's name and that lamb's just like 'im the way he puts his head down and gets stuck in, fearless like.'

I put my hand into the second ewe. Here was a glorious mix up of three lambs; little heads, legs, a tail, all fighting their way towards the outside world and effectively stopping each other from moving an inch.

'She's been hanging about all morning and painin'.' Rob said. 'I knew summat was wrong.'

Moving a hand carefully around the uterus I began the fascinating business of sorting out the tangle which is just about my favourite job in practice. I had to bring a head and two legs up together in order to deliver a lamb; but they had to belong to the same lamb or I was in trouble. It was a matter of tracing each leg back to see if it was hind or fore, to find if it joined the shoulder or disappeared into the depths.

After a few minutes I had a lamb assembled inside with his proper appendages but as I drew the legs into view the neck telescoped and the head slipped back; there was barely room for it to come through the pelvic bones along with the shoulders and I had to coax it through with a finger in the eye socket. This was groaningly painful as the bones squeezed my hand but only for a few seconds because the ewe gave a final strain and the little nose was visible. After that it was easy and I had him on the grass within seconds. The little creature gave a convulsive shake of his head and the farmer wiped him down quickly with straw before pushing him to his mother's head.

The ewe bent over him and began to lick his face and neck with little quick darts of her tongue; and she gave the deep chuckle of satisfaction that you hear from a sheep only at this time. The chuckling continued as I produced another pair of lambs from inside her, one of them hind end first, and, towelling my arms again, I watched her nosing round her triplets delightedly.

Soon they began to answer her with wavering, high-pitched cries and as I drew my coat thankfully over my cold-reddened arms, lamb numb number one began to struggle to his knees; he couldn't quite make it to his feet and kept toppling on to his face but he knew where he was going, all right; he was headed for that udder with a singleness of purpose which would soon be satisfied.

Despite the wind cutting over the straw bales into my face I found myself grinning down at the scene; this was always the best part, the wonder that was always fresh, the miracle you couldn't explain.

I heard from Rob Benson again a few days later. It was a Sunday afternoon and his voice was strained, almost panic stricken.

'Jim, I've had a dog in among me in-lamb ewes. There was some folk up here with a car about dinner time and my neighbour said they had an Alsatian and it was chasing the sheep all over the field. There's a hell of a mess — I tell you I'm frightened to look.'

'I'm on my way.' I dropped the receiver and hurried out to the car. I had a sinking dread of what would be waiting for me; the helpless animals lying with their throats torn, the terrifying lacerations of limbs and abdomen. I had seen it all before. The ones which didn't have to be slaughtered would need stitching and on the way I made a mental check of the stock of suture silk in the boot.

The in-lamb ewes were in a field by the roadside and my heart gave a quick thump as I looked over the wall; arms resting on the rough loose stones I gazed with sick dismay across the pasture. This was worse than I had feared. The long slope of turf was dotted with prostrate sheep — there must have been about fifty of them, motionless woolly mounds scattered at intervals on the green.

Rob was standing just inside the gate. He hardly looked at me. Just gestured with his head.

'Tell me what you think. I daren't go in there.'

I left him and began to walk among the stricken creatures, rolling them over, lifting their legs, parting the fleece of their necks to examine them. Some were completely unconscious, others comatose; none of them could stand up. But as I worked my way up the field I felt a growing bewilderment. Finally I called back to the farmer.

'Rob, come over here. There's something very strange.'

'Look,' I said as the farmer approached hesitantly. 'There's not a drop of blood nor a wound anywhere and yet all the sheep are flat out. I can't understand it.'

Rob bent over and gently raised a lolling head. 'Aye, you're right. What the hell's done it, then?'

At that moment I couldn't answer him, but a little bell was tinkling far away in the back of my mind. There was something familiar about that ewe the farmer had just handled. She was one of the few able to support herself on her chest and she was lying there, blank-eyed, oblivious of everything; but . . . that drunken nodding of the head, that watery nasal discharge . . . I had seen it before. I knelt down and as I put my face close to hers I heard a faint bubbling — almost a rattling — in her breathing. I knew then.

'It's calcium deficiency,' I cried and began to gallop down the slope towards the car.

Rob trotted alongside me. 'But what the 'ell? They get that after lambin', don't they?'

'Yes, usually,' I puffed. 'But sudden exertion and stress can bring it on.'

'Well ah never knew that,' panted Rob. 'How does it happen?'

I saved my breath. I wasn't going to start an exposition on the effects of sudden derangement of the parathyroid. I was more concerned with wondering if I had enough calcium in the boot for fifty ewes. It was reassuring to see the long row of round tin caps peeping from their cardboard box; I must have filled up recently.

I injected the first ewe in the vein just to check my diagnosis — calcium works as quickly as that in sheep — and felt a quiet elation as the unconscious animal began to blink and tremble, then tried to struggle on to its chest.

'We'll inject the others under the skin,' I said. 'It'll save time.

I began to work my way up the field. Rob pulled forward the fore leg of each sheep so that I could insert the needle under the convenient patch of unwoolled skin just behind the elbow; and by the time I was half way up the slope the ones at the bottom were walking about and getting their heads into the food troughs and hay racks.

It was one of the most satisfying experiences of my working life. Not clever, but a magical transfiguration; from despair to hope, from death to life within minutes.

I was throwing the empty bottles into the boot when Rob spoke. He was looking wonderingly up at the last of the ewes getting to its feet at the far end of the field.

'Well Jim, I'll tell you. I've never seen owt like that afore. But there's one thing bothers me.' He turned to me and his weathered features screwed up in puzzlement. 'Ah can understand how gettin' chased by a dog could affect some of them ewes, but why should the whole bloody lot go down?'

'Rob' I said. 'I don't know.'

And, thirty years later, I still wonder. I still don't know why the whole bloody lot went down.

I thought Rob had enough to worry about at the time, so I didn't point out to him that other complications could be expected after the Alsatian episode. I wasn't surprised when I had a call to the Benson farm within days.

I met him again on the hillside with the same wind whipping over the straw bale pens. The lambs had been arriving in a torrent and the noise was louder than ever. He led me to my patient.

'There's one with a bellyful of dead lambs, I reckon,' he said, pointing to a ewe with her head drooping, ribs heaving. She stood quite motionless and made no attempt to move away when I went up to her; this one was really sick and as the stink of decomposition came up to me I knew the farmer's diagnosis was right.

'Well I suppose it had to happen to one at least after that chasing round,' I said. 'Let's see what we can do, anyway.'

This kind of lambing is without charm but it has to be done to save the ewe. The lambs were putrid and distended with gas and I used a sharp scalpel to skin the legs to the shoulders so that I could remove them and deliver the little bodies with the least discomfort to the mother. When I had finished, the ewe's head was almost touching the ground, she was panting rapidly and grating her teeth. I had nothing to offer her — no wriggling new creature for her to lick and revive her interest in life. What she needed was an injection of penicillin, but this was 1939 and the antibiotics were still a little way round the corner.

'Well I wouldn't give much for her,' Rob grunted. 'Is there owt more you can do?'

'Oh, I'll put some pessaries in her and give her an injection, but what she needs most is a lamb to look after. You know as well as I do that ewes in this condition usually give up if they've nothing to occupy them. You haven't a spare lamb to put on her, have you?'

'Not right now, I haven't. And it's now she needs it. Tomorrow'll be too late.'

Just at that moment a familiar figure wandered into view. It was Herbert, the unwanted lamb, easily recognisable as he prowled from sheep to sheep in search of nourishment.

'Hey, do you think she'd take that little chap?' I asked the farmer.

He looked doubtful. 'Well I don't know — he's a bit old. Nearly a fortnight and they like 'em newly born.'

'But it's worth a try isn't it? Why not try the old trick on her?'

Rob grinned. 'O.K., we'll do that. There's nowt to lose. Anyway the little youth isn't much bigger than a new-born 'un. He hasn't grown as fast as his mates.' He took out his penknife and quickly skinned one of the dead lambs, then he tied the skin over Herbert's back and round his jutting ribs.

'Poor little bugger, there's nowt on 'im,' he muttered. 'If this doesn't work he's going in with the pet lambs.'

When he had finished he set Herbert on the grass and the lamb, resolute little character that he was, bored straight in under the sick ewe and began to suck. It seemed he wasn't having much success because he gave the udder a few peremptory thumps with his hard little head; then his tail began to wiggle.

'She's lettin' him have a drop, any road,' Rob laughed.

Herbert was a type you couldn't ignore and the big sheep, sick as she was, just had to turn her head for a look at him. She sniffed along the tied-on skin in a non-committal way then after a few seconds she gave a few quick licks and the merest beginning of the familiar deep chuckle.

I began to gather up my gear. 'I hope he makes it,' I said. 'Those two need each other.' As I left the pen Herbert, in his new jacket, was still working away.

For the next week I hardly seemed to have my coat on. The flood of sheep work was at its peak and I spent hours of every day with my arms in and out of buckets of hot water in all corners of the district — in the pens, in dark nooks in farm buildings or very often in the open fields, because the farmers of those days didn't find anything disturbing in the sight of a vet kneeling in his shirt sleeves for an hour in the rain.

I had one more visit to Rob Benson's place. To a ewe with a prolapsed uterus after lambing — a job whose chief delight was comparing it with the sweat of replacing a uterus in a cow.

It was so beautifully easy. Rob rolled the animal on to her side then held her more or less upside down by tying a length of rope to her hind legs and passing it round his neck. In that position she couldn't strain and I disinfected the organ and pushed it back with the minimum of effort, gently inserting an arm at the finish to work it properly into place.

Afterwards the ewe trotted away unperturbed with her family to join the rapidly growing flock whose din was all around us.

'Look!' Rob cried. 'There's that awd ewe with Herbert. Over there on t'right —

in the middle of that bunch.' They all looked the same to me but to Rob, like all shepherds, they were as different as people and he picked out these two effortlessly.

They were near the top of the field and as I wanted to have a close look at them we manoevered them into a corner. The ewe, fiercely possessive, stamped her foot at us as we approached, and Herbert, who had discarded his woolly jacket, held close to the flank of his new mother. He was, I noticed, faintly obese in appearance.

'You couldn't call him a runt now, Rob,' I said.

The farmer laughed. 'Nay, t'awd lass has a bag like a cow and Herbert's gettin' the lot. By gaw, he's in clover is that little youth and I reckon he saved the ewe's life — she'd have pegged out all right, but she never looked back once he came along.'

I looked away, over the noisy pens, over the hundreds of sheep moving across the fields. I turned to the farmer. 'I'm afraid you've seen a lot of me lately, Rob. I hope this is the last visit.'

'Aye well it could be. We're getting well through now . . . but it's a hell of a time, lambin', isn't it?'

'It is that. Well I must be off — I'll leave you to it.' I turned and made my way down the hillside, my arms raw and chafing in my sleeves, my cheeks whipped by the eternal wind gusting over the grass. At the gate I stopped and gazed back at the wide landscape, ribbed and streaked by the last of the winter's snow, and at the dark grey banks of cloud riding across on the wind followed by lakes of brightest blue; and in seconds the fields and walls and woods burst into vivid life and I had to close my eyes against the sun's glare. As I stood there the distant uproar came faintly down to me, the tumultuous harmony from deepest bass to highest treble; demanding, anxious, angry, loving.

The sound of the sheep, the sound of spring.

# Chapter 4

As the faint rumbling growl rolled up from the rib cage into the ear pieces of my stethoscope the realisation burst upon me with uncomfortable clarity that this was probably the biggest dog I had ever seen. In my limited past experience some Irish Wolfhounds had undoubtedly been taller and a certain number of Bull Mastiffs had possibly been broader, but for sheer gross poundage this one had it. His name was Clancy.

It was a good name for an Irishman's dog and Joe Mulligan was very Irish despite his many years in Yorkshire. Joe had brought him in to the afternoon surgery and as the huge hairy form ambled along, almost filling the passage, I was reminded of the times I had seen him out in the fields around Darrowby enduring the frisking attentions of smaller animals with massive benignity.

He looked like a nice friendly dog.

But now there was this ominous sound echoing round the great thorax like a distant drum roll in a subterranean cavern, and as the chest piece of the stethoscope bumped along the ribs the sound swelled in volume and the lips fluttered over the enormous teeth as though a gentle breeze had stirred them. It was then that I became aware not only that Clancy was very big indeed but that my position, kneeling on the floor with my right ear a few inches from his mouth, was infinitely vulnerable.

I got to my feet and as I dropped the stethoscope into my pocket the dog gave me a cold look — a sideways glance without moving his head; and there was a chilling menace in his very immobility. I didn't mind my patients snapping at me but this one, I felt sure, wouldn't snap. If he started something it would be on a spectacular scale.

I stepped back a pace. 'Now what did you say his symptoms were, Mr Mulligan?'

'Phwaat's that?' Joe cupped his ear

with his hand. I took a deep breath. 'What's the trouble with him?' I shouted.

The old man looked at me with total incomprehension from beneath the straightly adjusted cloth cap. He fingered the muffler knotted immediately over his larynx and the pipe which grew from the dead centre of his mouth puffed blue wisps of puzzlement.

Then, remembering something in Clancy's past history, I moved close to Mr Mulligan and bawled with all my power into his face. 'Is he vomiting?'

The response was immediate. Joe smiled in great relief and removed his pipe. 'Oh aye, he's womitin' sorr. He's womitin' bad.' Clearly he was on familiar ground.

Over the years Clancy's treatment had all been at long range. Siegfried had told me on the first day I had arrived in Darrowby two years ago that there was nothing wrong with the dog which he had described as a cross between an Airedale and a donkey, but his penchant for eating every bit of rubbish in his path had the inevitable result. A large bottle of bismuth, mag carb mixture had been dispensed at regular intervals. He had also told me that Clancy, when bored, used occasionally to throw Joe to the ground and worry him like a rat just for a bit of light relief. But his master still adored him.

Prickings of conscience told me I should carry out a full examination. Take his temperature, for instance. All I had to do was to grab hold of that tail, lift it and push a thermometer into his rectum. The dog turned his head and met my eye with a blank stare; again I heard the low booming drum roll and the upper lip lifted a fraction to show a quick gleam of white.

'Yes, yes, right, Mr Mulligan,' I said briskly. 'I'll get you a bottle of the usual.'

In the dispensary, under the rows of bottles with their Latin names and glass stoppers I shook up the mixture in a ten ounce bottle, corked it, stuck on a label and wrote the directions. Joe seemed well satisfied as he pocketed the familiar white medicine but as he turned to go my conscience smote me again. The dog did look perfectly fit but maybe he ought to be seen again.

'Bring him back again on Thursday afternoon at two o'clock,' I yelled into the old man's ear. 'And please come on time if you can. You were a bit late today.'

I watched Mr Mulligan going down the street, preceded by his pipe from which regular puffs rose upwards as though from a departing railway engine. Behind him ambled Clancy, a picture of massive calm. With his all-over covering of tight brown curls he did indeed look like a gigantic Airedale.

Thursday afternoon, I ruminated. That was my half day and at two o'clock I'd probably be watching the afternoon cinema show in Brawton.

The following Friday morning Siegfried was sitting behind his desk, working out the morning rounds. He scribbled a list of visits on a pad, tore out the sheet and handed it to me.

'Here you are, James, I think that'll just about keep you out of mischief till lunch time.' Then something in the previous day's entries caught his eye and he turned to his younger brother who was at his morning task of stoking the fire.

'Tristan, I see Joe Mulligan was in yesterday afternoon with his dog and you saw it. What did you make of it?'

Tristan put down his bucket. 'Oh, I gave him some of the bismuth mixture.'

'Yes, but what did your examination of the patient disclose?'

'Well now, let's see.' Tristan rubbed his chin. 'He looked pretty lively, really.'

'Is that all?'

'Yes . . . yes . . . I think so.'

Siegfried turned back to me. 'And how about you, James? You saw the dog the day before. What were your findings?'

'Well it was a bit difficult,' I said. 'That dog's as big as an elephant and there's something creepy about him. He seemed to me to be just waiting his chance and there was only old Joe to hold him. I'm afraid I wasn't able to make a close examination but I must say I thought the same as Tristan — he did look pretty lively.'

Siegfried put down his pen wearily. On the previous night, fate had dealt him one of the shattering blows which it occasionally reserves for vets — a call at each end of his sleeping time. He had been dragged from his bed at 1 a.m. and again at 6 a.m. and the fires of his personality were temporarily damped.

He passed a hand across his eyes. 'Well God help us. You, James, a veterinary surgeon of two years experience and you, Tristan, a final year student can't come up with anything better between you than the phrase "pretty lively". It's a bloody poor thing! Hardly a worthy description of clinical findings is it? When an animal comes in here I expect you to record pulse, temperature and respiratory rate. To auscultate the chest and thoroughly palpate the abdomen. To open his mouth and examine teeth gums and pharynx. To check the condition of the skin. To catheterise him and examine the urine if necessary.'

'Right,' I said.

'O.K.,' said Tristan.

My partner rose from his seat. 'Have you fixed another appointment?'

'I have, yes.' Tristan drew his packet of

Woodbines from his pocket. 'For Monday. And since Mr Mulligan's always late for the surgery I said we'd visit the dog at his home in the evening.'

'I see.' Siegfried made a note on the pad, then he looked up suddenly. 'That's when you and James are going to the young farmers' meeting, isn't it?'

The young man drew on his cigarette. 'That's right. Good for the practice for us to mix with the young clients.'

'Very well,' Siegfried said as he walked to the door. 'I'll see the dog myself.'

On the following Tuesday I was fairly confident that Siegfried would have something to say about Mulligan's dog, if only to point out the benefits of a thorough clinical examination. But he was silent on the subject.

It happened that I came upon old Joe in the market place sauntering over the cobbles with Clancy inevitably trotting at his heels.

I went up to him and shouted in his ear. 'How's your dog?'

Mr Mulligan removed his pipe and

smiled with slow benevolence. 'Oh foine, sorr, foine. Still vomitin' a bit, but not bad.'

Mr Farnon fixed him up, then?'

'Aye, gave him some more of the white medicine. It's wonderful stuff, sorr, wonderful stuff.'

'Good, good,' I said. 'He didn't find anything else when he examined him?'

Joe took another suck at his pipe. 'No he didn't now, he didn't. He's a clever man, Mr Farnon — I've niver seen a man work as fast, no I haven't.'

'What do you mean?'

'Well now he saw all he wanted in tree seconds, so he did.'

I was mystified. 'Three seconds?'

'Yes,' said Mr Mulligan firmly. 'Not a moment more.'

'Amazing. What happened?'

Joe tapped out his pipe on his heel and without haste took out a knife and began to carve a refill from an evil looking coil of black twist. 'Well now I'll tell ye. Mr Farnon is a man who moves awful sudden, and that night he banged on our front door and jumped into the room.' (I knew those cottages. There was no hall or lobby — you walked straight from the street into the living room.) 'And as he came in he was pullin' his thermometer out of its case. Well now Clancy was lyin' by the fire and he rose up in a flash and he gave a bit of a wuff, so he did.'

'A bit of a wuff, eh?' I could imagine the hairy monster leaping up and baying into Siegfried's face. I could see the gaping jaws, the gleaming teeth.

'Aye, just a bit of a wuff. Well, Mr Farnon just put the thermometer straight back in its case turned round and went out the door.'

'Didn't he say anything?' I asked.

'No, divil a word. Just turned about like a soldier and marched out the door, so he did.'

It sounded authentic. Siegfried was a man of instant decision. I put my hand out to pat Clancy but something in his eyes made me change my mind.

'Well, I'm glad he's better,' I shouted.

The old man ignited his pipe with an ancient brass lighter, puffed a cloud of choking blue smoke into my face and tapped a little metal lid on to the bowl. 'Aye, Mr Farnon sent round a big bottle of the white stuff and it's done 'im good. Mind yous,' he gave a beatific smile, 'Clancy's allus been one for the womitin', so he has.'

Nothing more was said about the big dog for over a week, but Siegfried's professional conscience must have been niggling at him because he came into the dispensary one afternoon when Tristan and I were busy at the tasks which have passed into history — making up fever drinks, stomach powders, boric acid pessaries. He was elaborately casual.

'Oh by the way, I dropped a note to Joe Mulligan. I'm not entirely convinced that we have adequately explored the causes of his dog's symptoms. This womiting . . . er, vomiting is almost certainly due to depraved appetite but I just want to make sure. So I have asked him to bring him round tomorrow afternoon between two and two thirty when we'll all be here.'

No cries of joy greeted his statement, so he continued. 'I suppose you could say that this dog is to some degree a difficult animal and I think we should plan accordingly.' He turned to me. 'James, when he arrives you get hold of his back end, will you?'

'Right', I replied without enthusiasm.

He faced his brother. 'And you, Tristan, can deal with the head. O.K.?'

'Fine, fine,' Tristan muttered, his face expressionless.

His brother continued. 'I suggest you get a good grip with your arms round his neck and I'll be ready to give him a shot of sedative.'

'Splendid, splendid,' said Tristan.

'Ah well, that's capital.' My partner rubbed his hands together. 'Once I get the dope into him the rest will be easy. I do like to satisfy my mind about these things.'

It was a typical Dales practice at Darrowby; mainly large animal and we didn't have packed waiting rooms at surgery times. But on the following afternoon we had nobody in at all, and it added to the tension of waiting. The three of us mooched about the office, making aimless conversation, glancing with studied carelessness into the front street, whistling little tunes to ourselves. By two twenty-five we had all fallen silent. Over the next five minutes we consulted our watches about every thirty seconds, then at exactly two thirty Siegfried spoke up.

'This is no damn good. I told Joe he had to be here before half past but he's taken not a bit of notice. He's always late and there doesn't seem to be any way to get him here on time.' He took a last look out of the window at the empty street. 'Right we're not waiting any longer. You and I, James, have got that colt to cut and you, Tristan, have to see that beast of Wilson's. So let's be off.'

Up till then, Laurel and Hardy were the only people I had ever seen getting jammed together in doorways but there was a moment when the three of us gave a passable imitation of the famous comics as we all fought our way into the passage at the same time. Within seconds we were in the street and Tristan was roaring off in a cloud of exhaust smoke. My colleague and I proceeded almost as rapidly in the opposite direction.

At the end of Trengate we turned into the market place and I looked around in vain for signs of Mr Mulligan. It wasn't until we had reached the outskirts of the town that we saw him. He had just left his house and was pacing along under a moving pall of blue smoke with Clancy as always bringing up the rear.

'There he is!' Siegfried exclaimed. 'Would you believe it? At the rate he's going he'll get to the surgery around three o'clock. Well we won't be there and it's his own fault.' He looked at the great curly-coated animal tripping along, a picture of health and energy. 'Well, I suppose we'd have been wasting our time examining that dog in any case. There's nothing really wrong with him.'

For a moment he paused, lost in thought, then he turned to me.

'He does look pretty lively, doesn't he?'

# Chapter 5

'Them masticks,' said Mr Pickersgill judicially, 'is a proper bugger.'

I nodded my head in agreement that his mastitis problem was indeed giving cause for concern; and reflected at the same time that while most farmers would have been content with the local word 'felon' it was typical that Mr Pickersgill should make a determined if somewhat inaccurate attempt at the scientific term.

He didn't usually go too far off the mark — most of his efforts were near misses or bore obvious evidence of their derivation — but I could never really fathom where he got the masticks. I did know that once he fastened on to an expression it never changed; mastitis had always been 'them masticks' with him and it always would be. And I knew, too, that nothing would ever stop him doggedly trying to be right. This, because Mr Pickersgill had what he considered to be a scholastic background. He was a man of about sixty and when in his teens he had attended a two week course of instruction for agricultural workers at Leeds University. This brief glimpse of the academic life had left an indelible impression on his mind, and it was as if the intimation of something deep and true behind the facts of his everyday work had kindled a flame in him which had illumined his subsequent life.

No capped and gowned don ever looked back to his years among the spires of Oxford with more nostalgia than did Mr Pickersgill to his fortnight at Leeds and his conversation was usually laced with references to a godlike Professor Malleson who had apparently been in charge of the course.

'Ah don't know what to make of it,' he continued. 'In ma college days I was allus told that you got a big swollen bag and dirty milk with them masticks but this must be another kind. Just little bits of flakes in the milk off and on — neither nowt nor something, but I'm right fed up with it, I'll tell you.'

I took a sip from the cup of tea which Mrs Pickersgill had placed in front of me on the kitchen table. 'Yes, it's very worrying the way it keeps going on and on. I'm sure there's a definite factor behind it all — I wish I could put my finger on it.'

But in fact I had a good idea what was behind it. I had happened in at the little byre late one afternoon when Mr Pickersgill and his daughter Olive were milking their ten cows. I had watched the two at work as they crouched under the row of roan and red backs and one thing was immediately obvious; while Olive drew the milk by almost imperceptible movements of her fingers and with a motionless wrist, her father hauled away at the teats as though he was trying to ring in the new year.

This insight coupled with the fact that it was always the cows Mr Pickersgill milked that gave trouble was enough to convince me that the chronic mastitis was of traumatic origin.

But how to tell the farmer that he wasn't doing his job right and that the only solution was to learn a more gentle technique or let Olive take over all the milking?

It wouldn't be easy because Mr. Pickersgill was an impressive man. I don't suppose he had a spare penny in the world but even as he sat there in the kitchen in his tattered, collarless flannel shirt and braces he looked, as always, like an industrial tycoon. You could imagine that massive head with its fleshy cheeks, noble brow and serene eyes looking out from the financial pages of the Times. Put him in a bowler and striped trousers and you'd have the perfect chairman of the board.

I was very chary of affronting such natural dignity and anyway, Mr Pickersgill was fundamentally a fine stocksman. His few cows, like all the animals of that fast-dying breed of small farmer, were fat and sleek and clean. You had to look after your beasts when they were your only source of income and somehow Mr Pickersgill had brought up a family by milk production eked out by selling a few pigs and the eggs from his wife's fifty hens.

I could never quite work out how they did it but they lived, and they lived graciously. All the family but Olive had married and left home but there was still a rich decorum and harmony in that house. The present scene was typical. The farmer expounding gravely, Mrs Pickersgill bustling about in the background, listening to him with quiet pride. Olive, too, was happy. Though in her late thirties, she had no fears of spinsterhood because she had been assiduously courted for fifteen years by Charlie Hudson from the Darrowby fish shop and though Charlie was not a tempestuous suitor there was nothing flighty about him and he was confidently expected to pop the question over the next ten years or so.

Mr Pickersgill offered me another buttered scone and when I declined he cleared his throat a few times as though trying to find words. 'Mr Herriot,' he said at last, 'I don't like to tell nobody his job, but we've tried all your remedies for them masticks and we've still got trouble.

Now when I studied under Professor Malleson I noted down a lot of good cures and I'd like to try this 'un. Have a look at it.'

He put his hand in his hip pocket and produced a yellowed slip of paper almost falling apart at the folds. 'It's an udder salve. Maybe if we gave the bags a good rub with it it'd do t'trick.'

I read the prescription in the fine copperplate writing. Camphor, eucalyptus, zinc oxide — a long list of the old familiar names. I couldn't help feeling a kind of affection for them but it was tempered by a growing disillusion. I was about to say that I didn't think rubbing anything on the udder would make the slightest difference when the farmer groaned loudly.

The action of reaching into his hip pocket had brought on a twinge of his lumbago and he sat very upright, grimacing with pain.

'This bloody old back of mine! By gaw, it does give me some stick, and the doctor can't do nowt about it. I've had enough pills to make me rattle but ah get no relief.'

I'm not brilliant but I do get the odd blinding flash and I had one now.

'Mr Pickersgill,' I said solemnly, 'You've suffered from that lumbago ever since I've known you and I've just thought of something. I believe I know how to cure it.'

The farmer's eyes widened and he stared at me with a childlike trust in which there was no trace of scepticism. This could be expected, because just as people place more reliance on the words of knacker men and meal travellers than their vets' when their animals are concerned it was natural that they would believe the vet rather than their doctor with their own ailments.

'You know how to put me right?' he said faintly.

'I think so, and it has nothing to do with medicine. You'll have to stop milking.'

'Stop milking! What the 'ell. . . ?'

'Of course. Don't you see, it's sitting crouched on that little stool night and morning every day of the week that's doing it. You're a big chap and you've got to bend to get down there — I'm sure it's bad for you.'

Mr Pickersgill gazed into space as though he had seen a vision. 'You really think . . .'

'Yes, I do. You ought to give it a try, anyway. Olive can do the milking. She's always saying she ought to do it all.'

'That's right, Dad,' Olive chimed in. 'I like milking, you know I do, and it's time you gave it up — you've done it ever since you were a lad.'

'Dang it, young man, I believe you're right! I'll pack it in, now — I've made my decision!' Mr Pickersgill threw up his fine head, looked imperiously around him and crashed his fist on the table as though he had just concluded a merger between two oil companies.

I stood up. 'Fine, fine. I'll take this prescription with me and make up the udder salve. It'll be ready for you tonight and I should start using it immediately.'

It was about a month later that I saw Mr Pickersgill. He was on a bicycle, pedalling majestically across the market place and he dismounted when he saw me.

'Now then, Mr Herriot,' he said, puffing slightly. 'I'm glad I've met you. I've been meaning to come and tell you that we don't have no flakes in the milk now. Ever since we started with t'salve they began to disappear and milk's as clear as it can be now.'

'Oh, great. And how's your lumbago?'

'Well I'll tell you, you've really capped it and I'm grateful. Ah've never milked since that day and I hardly get a twinge now.' He paused and smiled indulgently. 'You gave me some good advice for me back, but we had to go back to awd Professor Malleson to cure them masticks, didn't we?'

My next encounter with Mr Pickersgill was on the telephone.

'I'm speaking from the cossack,' he said in a subdued shout.

'From the what?'

'The cossack, the telephone cossack in t'village.'

'Yes indeed,' I said, 'And what can I do for you?'

'I want you to come out as soon as

75

possible, to treat a calf for semolina.'

'I beg your pardon?'

'I 'ave a calf with semolina.'

'Semolina?'

'Aye, that's right. A feller was on about it on t'wireless the other morning.'

'Oh! Ah yes, I see.' I too had heard a bit of the farming talk on Salmonella infection in calves. 'What makes you think you've got this trouble?'

'Well it's just like that feller said. Me calf's bleeding from the rectrum.'

'From the. . . ? Yes, yes, of course. Well I'd better have a look at him — I won't be long.'

The calf was pretty ill when I saw him and he did have rectal bleeding, but it wasn't like Salmonella.

'There's no diarrhoea, you see, Mr Pickersgill,' I said. 'In fact, he seems to be constipated. This is almost pure blood coming away from him. And he hasn't got a very high temperature.'

The farmer seemed a little disappointed. 'Dang, I thowt it was just same as that feller was talking about. He said you could send samples off to the labrador.'

'Eh? To the what?'

'The investigation labrador — you know.'

'Oh yes, quite, but I don't think the lab would be of any help in this case.'

'Aye well, what's wrong with him, then? Is something the matter with his rectrum?'

'No, no,' I said. 'But there seems to be some obstruction high up his bowel which is causing this haemorrhage.' I looked at the little animal standing motionless with his back up. He was totally preoccupied with some internal discomfort and now and then he strained and grunted softly.

And of course I should have known straight away — it was so obvious. But I suppose we all have blind spells when we can't see what is pushed in front of our eyes, and for a few days I played around with that calf in a haze of ignorance, giving it this and that medicine which I'd rather not talk about.

But I was lucky. He recovered in spite of my treatment. It wasn't until Mr Pickersgill showed me the little roll of necrotic tissue which the calf had passed that the thing dawned on me.

I turned, shame-faced, to the farmer. 'This is a bit of dead bowel all telescoped together — an intussusception. It's usually a fatal condition but fortunately in this case the obstruction has sloughed away and your calf should be all right now.'

'What was it you called it?'

'An intussusception.'

Mr Pickersgill's lips moved tentatively and for a moment I thought he was going to have a shot at it. But he apparently decided against it. 'Oh,' he said. 'That's what it was, was it?'

'Yes, and it's difficult to say just what caused it.'

The farmer sniffed. 'I'll bet I know what was behind it. I always said this one 'ud be a weakly calf. When he was born he bled a lot from his biblical cord.'

Mr Pickersgill hadn't finished with me yet. It was only a week later that I heard him on the phone again.

'Get out here, quick. There's one of me pigs going bezique.'

'Bezique?' With an effort I put away from me a mental picture of two porkers facing each other over a green baize table. 'I'm afraid I don't quite . . .''

'Aye, ah gave him a dose of worm medicine and he started jumpin' about and rollin' on his back. I tell you he's going proper bezique.'

'Ah! Yes, yes I see, right. I'll be with you in a few minutes.'

The pig had quieted down a bit when I arrived but was still in a considerable pain, getting up, lying down, trotting in spurts round the pen. I gave him half a grain of morphine hydrochloride as a sedative and within a few minutes he began to relax and finally curled up in the straw.

'Looks as though he's going to be all right,' I said. 'But what's this worm medicine you gave him?'

Mr Pickersgill produced the bottle sheepishly.

'Bloke was coming round sellin' them. Said it would shift any worms you cared to name.'

'It nearly shifted your pig, didn't it?' I

sniffed at the mixture. 'And no wonder. It smells almost like pure turpentine.'

'Turpentine! Well by gaw is that all it is? And bloke said it was summat new. Charged me an absorbent price for it too.'

I gave him back the bottle. 'Well never mind, I don't think there's any harm done, but I think the dustbin's the best place for that.'

As I was getting into my car I looked up at the farmer. 'You must be about sick of the sight of me. First the mastitis, then the calf and now your pig. You've had a bad run.'

Mr Pickersgill squared his shoulders and gazed at me with massive composure. Again I was conscious of the sheer presence of the man.

'Young feller,' he said. 'That don't bother me. When there's stock there's trouble and ah know from experience that trouble allus comes in cyclones.'

# Chapter 6

I knew I shouldn't do it, but the old Drovers' Road beckoned to me irresistibly. I ought to be hurrying back to the surgery after my morning call but the broad green path wound beguilingly over the moor top between its crumbling walls and almost before I knew, I was out of the car and treading the wiry grass.

The wall skirted the hill's edge and as I looked across and away to where Darrowby huddled far below between its folding green fells the wind thundered in my ears; but when I squatted in the shelter of the grey stones the wind was only a whisper and the spring sunshine hot on my face. The best kind of sunshine — not heavy or cloying but clear and bright and clean as you find it down behind a wall in Yorkshire with the wind singing over the top.

I slid lower till I was stretched on the

turf, gazing with half closed eyes into the bright sky, luxuriating in the sensation of being detached from the world and its problems.

This form of self-indulgence had become part of my life and still is; a reluctance to come down from the high country; a penchant for stepping out of the stream of life and loitering on the brink for a few minutes as an uninvolved spectator.

And it was easy to escape, lying up here quite alone with no sound but the wind sighing and gusting over the empty miles and, far up in the wide blue, the endless brave trilling of the larks.

Not that there was anything unpleasant about going back down the hill to Darrowby even before I was married. I had worked there for two years before Helen arrived, and Skeldale House had become home and the two bright minds in it my friends. It didn't bother me that both the brothers were cleverer than I was. Siegfried — unpredictable, explosive, generous; I had been lucky to have him as a partner. As a city bred youth trying to tell expert stock farmers how to treat their animals I had needed all his skill and guidance behind me. And Tristan; a rum lad as they said, but very sound. His humour and zest for life had lightened my days.

And all the time I was adding practical experience to my theory. The mass of facts I had learned at college were all coming to life, and there was the growing realisation, deep and warm, that this was for me. There was nothing else I'd rather do.

It must have been fifteen minutes later when I finally rose, stretched pleasurably, took a last deep gulp of the crisp air and pottered slowly back to the car for the six mile journey back down the hill to Darrowby.

When I drew up by the railings with Siegfried's brass plate hanging lopsidedly atop mine by the fine Georgian doorway I looked up at the tall old house with the ivy swarming untidily over the weathered brick. The white paint on windows and doors was flaking and that ivy needed trimming but the whole place had style, a serene unchangeable grace.

But I had other things on my mind at the moment. I went inside, stepping quietly over the coloured tiles which covered the floor of the long passage till I reached the long offshoot at the back of the house. And I felt as I always did the subdued excitement as I breathed the smell of our trade which always hung there; ether, carbolic and pulv aromat. The latter was the spicy powder which we mixed with the cattle medicines to make them more palatable and it had a distinctive bouquet which even now can take me back thirty years with a single sniff.

And today the thrill was stronger than usual because my visit was of a surreptitious nature. I almost tiptoed along the last stretch of passage, dodged quickly round the corner and into the dispensary. Gingerly I opened the cupboard door at one end and pulled out a little drawer. I was pretty sure Siegfried had a spare hoof knife hidden away within and I had to suppress a cackle of triumph when I saw it lying there; almost brand new with a nicely turned gleaming blade and a polished wooden handle.

My hand was outstretched to remove it when a cry of anger exploded in my right ear.

'Caught in the act! Bloody red-handed, by God!' Siegfried, who had apparently shot up through the floorboards, was breathing fire into my face.

The shock was so tremendous that the instrument dropped from my trembling fingers and I cowered back against a row of bottles of formalin bloat mixture.

'Oh hello, Siegfried,' I said with a ghastly attempt at nonchalance. 'Just on my way to that horse of Thompson's. You know — the one with the pus in the foot. I seem to have mislaid my knife so I thought I'd borrow this one.'

'Thought you'd nick it, you mean! My spare hoof knife! By heaven, is nothing sacred, James?'

I smiled sheepishly. 'Oh you're wrong. I'd have given it back to you straight away.'

'A likely story!' Siegfried said with a bitter smile. 'I'd never have seen it again and you know damn well I wouldn't.

Anyway, where's your own knife? You've left it on some farm, haven't you?'

'Well as a matter of fact I laid it down at Willie Denholm's place after I'd finished trimming his cow's overgrown foot and I must have forgotten to pick it up.' I gave a light laugh.

'But God help us, James, you're always forgetting to pick things up. And you're always making up the deficiency by purloining my equipment.' He stuck his chin out. 'Have you any idea how much all this is costing me?'

'Oh but I'm sure Mr Denholm will drop the knife in at the surgery the first time he's in town.'

Siegfried nodded gravely. 'He may, I'll admit that, he may. But on the other hand he might think it is the ideal tool for cutting up his plug tobacco. Remember when you left your calving overall at old Fred Dobson's place? The next time I saw it was six months later and Fred was wearing it. He said it was the best thing he'd ever found for stooking corn in wet weather.'

'Yes, I remember. I'm really sorry

about it all.' I fell silent, breathing in the pungency of the pulv aromat. Somebody had let a bagful burst on the floor and the smell was stronger than ever.

My partner kept his fiery gaze fixed on me for a few moments more then he shrugged his shoulders. 'Ah well, there's none of us perfect, James. And I'm sorry I shouted at you. But you know I'm deeply attached to that knife and this business of leaving things around is getting under my skin.' He took down a Winchester of his favourite colic draught and polished it with his handkerchief before replacing it carefully on its shelf. 'I tell you what, let's go and sit down for a few minutes and talk about this problem.'

We went back along the passage and as I followed him into the big sitting room Tristan got up from his favourite chair and yawned deeply. His face looked as boyish and innocent as ever but the lines of exhaustion round his eyes and mouth told an eloquent story. Last night he had travelled with the darts team from the Lord Nelson and had taken part in a gruelling match against the Dog and Gun at Drayton. The contest had been followed by a pie and peas supper and the consumption of something like twelve pints of bitter a man. Tristan had crawled into bed at 3 a.m. and was clearly in a delicate condition.

'Ah, Tristan,' Siegfried said. 'I'm glad you're here because what I have to say concerns you just as much as James. It's about leaving instruments on farms and you're as guilty as he is.' (It must be remembered that before the Veterinary Surgeons' act of 1948 it was quite legal for students to treat cases and they regularly did so. Tristan in fact had done much sterling work when called on and was very popular with the farmers.)

'Now I mean this very seriously,' my partner said, leaning his elbow on the mantelpiece and looking from one of us to the other. 'You two are bringing me to the brink of ruin by losing expensive equipment. Some of it is returned but a lot of it is never seen again. What's the use of sending you to visits when you come back without your artery forceps or scissors or something else? The profit's gone, you see?

We nodded silently.

'After all, there's nothing difficult about bringing your instruments away, is there? You may wonder why I never leave anything behind — well I can tell you it's just a matter of concentration. When I lay a thing down I always impress on my mind that I've got to lift it up again. That's all there is to it.'

The lecture over, he became very brisk. 'Right, let's get on. There's nothing much doing, James, so I'd like you to come with me to Kendall's of Brookside. He's got a few jobs including a cow with a tumour to remove. I don't know the details but we may have to cast her. You can go on to Thompson's later.' He turned to his brother. 'And you'd better come too, Tristan. I don't know if we'll need you but an extra man might come in handy.'

We made quite a procession as we trooped into the farm yard and Mr Kendall met us with his customary ebullience.

'Hello, 'ello, we've got plenty of man power today, I see. We'll be able to tackle owt with this regiment.'

Mr Kendall had the reputation in the district of being a 'bit clever' and the phrase has a different meaning in Yorkshire from elsewhere. It meant he was something of a know-all; and the fact that he considered himself a wag and legpuller of the first degree didn't endear him to his fellow farmers either.

I always felt he was a good-hearted man, but his conviction that he knew everything and had seen it all before made him a difficult man to impress.

'Well what d'you want to see first, Mr Farnon?' he asked. He was a thick-set little man with a round, smooth-skinned face and mischievous eyes.

'I believe you have a cow with a bad eye,' Siegfried said. 'Better begin with that.'

'Right squire,' the farmer cried, then he put his hand in his pocket. 'But before we start, here's something for you.' He pulled forth a stethoscope. 'You left it last time you were 'ere.'

There was a silence, then Siegfried grunted a word of thanks and grabbed it hastily from his hand.

Mr Kendall continued. 'And the time afore that you left your bloodless castrators. We did a swop over, didn't we? I gave you back the nippers and you left me the earphones.' He burst into a peal of laughter.

'Yes, yes, quite,' Siegfried snapped, glancing uneasily round at us, 'but we must be getting on. Where is . . . ?'

'You know lads,' chuckled the farmer, turning to us. 'Ah don't think I've ever known 'im come here without leaving summat.'

'Really?' said Tristan interestedly.

'Aye, if I'd wanted to keep 'em all I'd have had a drawerful by now.'

'Is that so?' I said.

'Aye it is, young man. And it's the same with all me neighbours. One feller said to me t'other day. "He's a kind man is Mr Farnon — never calls without leavin' a souvenir." ' He threw back his head and laughed again.

We were enjoying the conversation but my partner was stalking up the byre. 'Where's this damn cow, Mr Kendall? We

91

haven't got all day.'

The patient wasn't hard to find; a nice light roan cow which looked round at us carefully one eye almost closed. From between the lashes a trickle of tears made a dark stain down the hair of the face, and there was an eloquent story of pain in the cautious movements of the quivering lids.

'There's something in there,' murmured Siegfried.

'Aye, ah know!' Mr Kendall always knew. 'She's got a flippin' great lump of chaff stuck on her eyeball but I can't get to it. Look here.' He grabbed the cow's nose with one hand and tried to prise the eyelids apart with the fingers of the other, but the third eyelid came across and the whole orbit rolled effortlessly out of sight leaving only a blank expanse of white sclera.

'There!' he cried. 'Nowt to see. You can't make her keep her eye still.'

'I can, though.' Siegfried turned to his brother. 'Tristan, get the chloroform muzzle from the car. Look sharp!'

The young man was back in seconds and Siegfried quickly drew the canvas bag over the cow's face and buckled it behind the ears. From a bottle of spirit he produced a small pair of forceps of an unusual type with tiny jaws operated by a spring. He poised them just over the closed eye.

'James,' he said, 'Give her about an ounce.'

I dribbled the chloroform on to the sponge in the front of the muzzle. Nothing happened for a few moments while the animal took a few breaths then her eyes opened wide in surprise as the strange numbing vapour rolled into her lungs.

The whole area of the affected eye was displayed, with a broad golden piece of chaff splayed out across the dark cornea. I only had a glimpse of it before Siegfried's little forceps had seized it and whisked it away.

'Squeeze in some of that ointment, Tristan,' said my partner. 'And get the muzzle off, James, before she starts to rock.'

With the bag away from her face and the tormenting little object gone from her eye the cow looked around her, vastly relieved. The whole thing had taken only a minute or two and was as slick a little exhibition as you'd wish to see, but Mr Kendall didn't seem to think a great deal of it.

'Aye right,' he grunted. 'Let's get on with t'next job.'

As we went down the byre I looked out and saw a horse being led across the yard. Siegfried pointed to it.

'Is that the gelding I operated on for fistulous withers?' he asked.

'That's the one.' The farmer's voice was airy.

We went out and Siegfried ran his hand over the horse's shoulders. The broad fibrous scar over the withers was all that was left of the discharging, stinking sinus of a few weeks back. Healing was perfect. These cases were desperately difficult to treat and I remembered my partner cutting and chiselling at the mass of necrotic tissue, curetting deeply till only healthy flesh and bone remained. His efforts had been rewarded; it was a brilliant success.

Siegfried gave the gelding a final pat on

the neck. 'That's done rather well.'

Mr Kendall shrugged and turned back towards the byre. 'Aye, not so bad, I suppose.' But he really wasn't impressed.

The cow with the tumour was standing just inside the door. The growth was in the perineal region, a smooth round object like an apple projecting from the animal's rear end, clearly visible an inch to the right of the tail.

Mr Kendall was in full cry again. 'Now we'll see what you're made of. How are you chaps going to get that thing off, eh? It's a big 'un — you'll need a carving knife or a hack saw for t'job. And are you goin' to put her to sleep or tie her up or what?' He grinned and his bright little eyes darted at each of us in turn.

Siegfried reached out and grasped the tumour, feeling round the base with his fingers. 'Hmm . . . yes . . . hmm . . . bring me some soap and water and a towel, will you please?'

'I have it just outside t'door.' The farmer scuttled into the yard and back again with the bucket.

'Thank you very much,' Siegfried said.

He washed his hands and gave them a leisurely towelling. 'Now I believe you have another case to see. A scouring calf, wasn't it?'

The farmer's eyes widened. 'Yes, I 'ave. But how about getting this big lump off the cow first?'

Siegfried folded the towel and hung it over the half door. 'Oh, I've removed the tumour,' he said quietly.

'What's that?' Mr Kendall stared at the cow's backside. We all stared at it. And there was no doubt about it — the growth was gone. And there was another funny thing — there wasn't even a scar or mark remaining. I was standing quite close to the animal and I could see exactly to a fraction of an inch where that big ugly projection had been; and there was nothing, not a drop of blood, nothing.

'Aye,' Mr Kendall said irresolutely. 'You've er . . . you've removed . . . you've removed it, aye, that's right.' The smile had vanished from his face and his entire personality seemed suddenly deflated. Being a man who knew everything and was surprised by nothing he was unable to say, 'When the devil did you do it? And how? And what on earth have you done with it?' He had to maintain face at all costs, but he was rattled. He darted little glances around the byre, along the channel. The cow was standing in a clean-swept stall with no straw and there was nothing lying on the floor there or anywhere. Casually, as though by accident, he pushed a milking stool to one side with his foot — still nothing.

'Well now, perhaps we can see the calf.' Siegfried began to move away.

Mr Kendall nodded. 'Yes . . . yes . . . the calf. He's in t'corner there. I'll just lift bucket first.'

It was a blatant excuse. He went over to the bucket and as he passed behind the cow he whipped out his spectacles, jammed them on his nose and directed a piercing glare at the cow's bottom. He only took an instant because he didn't want to show undue concern, but when he turned back towards us his face registered utter despair and he put his spectacles away with a weary gesture of defeat.

As he approached I turned and brushed against my partner.

'Where the hell is it?' I hissed.

'Up my sleeve,' murmured Siegfried without moving his lips or changing expression.

'What. . . ?' I began, but Siegfried was climbing over a gate into the makeshift pen where the calf was cornered.

He was in expansive mood as he examined the little creature and injected it. He kept up a steady flow of light conversation and Mr Kendall, showing great character, managed to get his smile back on and answer back. But his preoccupied manner, the tortured eyes and the repeated incredulous glances back along the byre floor in the direction of the cow betrayed the fact that he was under immense strain.

Siegfried didn't hurry over the calf and when he had finished he lingered a while in the yard, chatting about the weather, the way the grass was springing, the price of fat bullocks.

Mr Kendall hung on grimly but by the time Siegfried finally waved farewell the farmer's eyes were popping and his face was an anguished mask. He bolted back into the byre and as the car backed round I could see him bent double with his glasses on again, peering into the corners.

'Poor fellow,' I said. 'He's still looking for that thing. And for God's sake where is it, anyway?'

'I told you, didn't I?' Siegfried removed one arm from the wheel and shook it. A round fleshy ball rolled down into his hand.

I stared at it in amazement. 'But . . . I never saw you take it off . . . what happened?'

'I'll tell you.' My partner smiled indulgently. 'I was fingering it over to see how deeply it was attached when I felt it begin to move. The back of it was merely encapsulated by the skin and when I gave another squeeze it just popped out and shot up my sleeve. And after it had gone the lips of the skin sprang back together again so that you couldn't see where it had been. Extraordinary thing.'

Tristan reached over from the back seat. 'Give it to me,' he said. 'I'll take it back to college with me and get it sectioned. We'll find out what kind of tumour it is.'

His brother smiled. 'Yes, I expect they'll give it some fancy name, but I'll always remember it as the only thing that shook Mr Kendall.'

'That was an interesting session in there,' I said. 'And I must say I admired the way you dealt with that eye, Siegfried. Very smooth indeed.'

'You're very kind, James,' my partner murmured. 'That was just one of my little tricks — and of course the forceps helped a lot.'

I nodded. 'Yes, wonderful little things. I've never seen anything like them. Where did you get them?'

'Picked them up on an instrument stall at the last Veterinary Congress. They cost me a packet but they've been worth it. Here, let me show them to you.' He put his hand in his breast pocket, then his side pockets, and as he continued to rummage all over his person a look of sick dismay spread slowly across his face.

Finally he abandoned the search,

cleared his throat and fixed his eyes on the road ahead.

'I'll er . . . I'll show you them some other time, James,' he said huskily.

I didn't say anything but I knew and Siegfried knew and Tristan knew.

He'd left them on the farm.

# Chapter 7

One of the nicest things about my married life was that my new wife got on so well with the Farnon brothers. And this was fitting because both of them had done their utmost to further my suit, Siegfried by means of some well-timed kicks in the pants, Tristan by more subtle motivation. The young man had been reassuring when I consulted him in the dispensary about my wooing that early summer morning.

'Well, it's a good sign.' Tristan reluctantly expelled a lungful of Woodbine smoke and looked at me with wide, encouraging eyes.

'You think so?' I said doubtfully.

Tristan nodded. 'Sure of it. Helen just rang you up, did she?'

'Yes, out of the blue. I haven't seen her since I took her to the pictures that night and it's been hectic ever since with the lambing — and suddenly there she was asking me to tea on Sunday.'

'I like the sound of it,' Tristan said. 'But of course you don't want to get the idea you're home and dry or anything like that. You know there are others in the field?'

'Hell, yes, I suppose I'm one of a crowd.'

'Not exactly, but Helen Alderson is really something. Not just a looker but . . . mm-mm, very nice. There's a touch of class about that girl.'

'Oh I know, I know. There's bound to be a mob of blokes after her. Like young Richard Edmundson — I hear he's very well placed.'

'That's right,' Tristan said. 'Old friends of the family, big farmers, rolling in brass. I understand old man Alderson fancies Richard strongly as a son-in-law.'

I dug my hands into my pockets. 'Can't blame him. A ragged arsed young vet isn't much competition.'

'Well, don't be gloomy, old boy, you've made a bit of progress, haven't you?'

'In a way,' I said with a wry smile. 'I've taken her out twice — to a dinner dance which wasn't on and to a cinema showing

103

the wrong film. A dead loss the first time and not much better the second. I just don't seem to have any luck there — something goes wrong every time. Maybe this invitation is just a polite gesture — returning hospitality or something like that.'

'Nonsense!' Tristan laughed and patted me on the shoulder. 'This is the beginning of better things. You'll see — nothing will go wrong this time.'

And on Sunday afternoon as I got out of the car to open the gate to Heston Grange it did seem as if all was right with the world. The rough track snaked down from the gate through the fields to Helen's home slumbering in the sunshine by the curving river, and the grey-stoned old building was like a restful haven against the stark backcloth of the fells beyond.

I leaned on the gate for a moment, breathing in the sweet air. There had been a change during the last week; the harsh winds had dropped, everything had softened and greened and the warming land gave off its scents. On the lower slopes of the fell, in the shade of the pine woods, a pale mist of bluebells drifted among the dead bronze of the bracken and their fragrance came up to me on the breeze.

I drove down the track among the cows relishing the tender young grass after their long winter in the byres and as I knocked on the farmhouse door I felt a surge of optimism and well-being. Helen's younger sister answered and it wasn't until I walked into the big flagged kitchen that I experienced a qualm. Maybe it was because it was so like that first disastrous time I had called for Helen; Mr Alderson was there by the fireside, deep in the Farmer and Stockbreeder as before, while above his head the cows in the vast oil painting still paddled in the lake of startling blue under the shattered peaks. On the whitewashed wall the clock still tick-tocked inexorably.

Helen's father looked up over his spectacles just as he had done before. 'Good afternoon, young man, come and sit down.' And as I dropped into the chair opposite to him he looked at me uncertainly for a few seconds. 'It's a better day,' he murmured, then his eyes were drawn back irresistibly to the pages on his knee. As he bent his head and started to read again I gained the strong impression that he hadn't the slightest idea who I was.

It came back to me forcibly that there was a big difference in coming to a farm as a vet and visiting socially. I was often in farm kitchens on my rounds, washing my hands in the sink after kicking my boots off in the porch, chatting effortlessly to the farmer's wife about the sick beast. But here I was in my good suit sitting stiffly across from a silent little man whose daughter I had come to court. It wasn't the same at all.

I was relieved when Helen came in carrying a cake which she placed on the big table. This wasn't easy as the table was already loaded; ham and egg pies rubbing shoulders with snowy scones, a pickled tongue cheek by jowl with a bowl of mixed salad, luscious looking custard tarts jockeying for position with sausage rolls, tomato sandwiches, fairy cakes. In

106

a clearing near the centre a vast trifle reared its cream-topped head. It was a real Yorkshire tea.

Helen came over to me. 'Hello, Jim, it's nice to see you — you're quite a stranger.' She smiled her slow, friendly smile.

'Hello, Helen. Yes, you know what lambing time's like. I hope things will ease up a bit now.'

'Well I hope so too. Hard work's all right up to a point but you need a break some time. Anyway, come and have some tea. Are you hungry?'

'I am now,' I said, gazing at the packed foodstuffs. Helen laughed. 'Well come on, sit in. Dad, leave your precious Farmer and Stockbreeder and come over here. We were going to sit you in the dining room, Jim, but Dad won't have his tea anywhere but in here, so that's all about it.'

I took my place along with Helen, young Tommy and Mary her brother and sister, and Auntie Lucy, Mr Alderson's widowed sister who had recently come to live with the family. Mr Alderson groaned his way over the flags, collapsed onto a high-backed wooden chair and began to saw

107

phlegmatically at the tongue.

As I accepted my laden plate I can't say I felt entirely at ease. In the course of my work I had eaten many meals in the homes of the hospitable Dalesmen and I had discovered that light chatter was not welcomed at table. The accepted thing, particularly among the more old-fashioned types, was to put the food away in silence and get back on the job, but maybe this was different. Sunday tea might be a more social occasion; I looked round the table, waiting for somebody to lead the way.

Helen spoke up. 'Jim's had a busy time among the sheep since we saw him last.'

'Oh yes?' Auntie Lucy put her head on one side and smiled. She was a little bird-like woman, very like her brother and the way she looked at me made me feel she was on my side.

The young people regarded me fixedly with twitching mouths. The only other time I had met them they had found me an object of some amusement and things didn't seem to have changed. Mr Alderson sprinkled some salt on a radish, conveyed it to his mouth and crunched it impassively.

'Did you have much twin lamb disease this time, Jim?' Helen asked, trying again.

'Quite a bit,' I replied brightly. 'Haven't had much luck with treatment, though. I tried dosing the ewes with glucose this year and I think it did a bit of good.'

Mr Alderson swallowed the last of his radish. 'I think nowt to glucose,' he grunted. 'I've had a go with it and I think nowt to it.'

'Really?' I said. 'Well now that's interesting. Yes . . . yes . . . quite.'

I buried myself in my salad for a spell before offering a further contribution.

'There's been a lot of sudden deaths in the lambs,' I said. 'Seems to be more Pulpy Kidney about.'

'Fancy that,' said Auntie Lucy, smiling encouragingly.

'Yes,' I went on, getting into my stride. 'It's a good job we've got a vaccine against it now.'

'Wonderful things, those vaccines,' Helen chipped in. 'You'll soon be able to prevent a lot of the sheep diseases that way.' The conversation was warming up.

Mr Alderson finished his tongue and pushed his plate away. 'I think nowt to the vaccines. And those sudden deaths you're on about — they're caused by wool ball on t'stomach. Nowt to do wi' the kidneys.'

'Ah yes, wool ball eh? I see, wool ball.' I subsided and decided to concentrate on the food.

And it was worth concentrating on. As I worked my way through I was aware of a growing sense of wonder that Helen had probably baked the entire spread. It was when my teeth were sinking into a poem of a curd tart that I really began to appreciate the miracle that somebody of Helen's radiant attractiveness should be capable of this.

I looked across at her. She was a big girl, nothing like her little wisp of a father. She must have taken after her mother. Mrs Alderson had been dead for many years and I wondered if she had had that same wide, generous mouth that smiled so easily, those same warm blue eyes under the soft mass of black-brown hair.

A spluttering from Tommy and Mary showed that they had been appreciately observing me gawping at their sister.

'That's enough, you two,' Auntie Lucy reproved. 'Anyway you can go now, we're going to clear the table.'

Helen and she began to move the dishes to the scullery beyond the door while Mr Alderson and I returned to our chairs by the fireside.

The little man ushered me to mine with a vague wave of the hand. 'Here . . . take a seat, er . . . young man.'

A clattering issued from the kitchen as the washing-up began. We were alone.

Mr Alderson's hand strayed automatically towards his Farmer and Stockbreeder but he withdrew it after a single hunted glance in my direction and began to drum his fingers on the arm of the chair, whistling softly under his breath.

I groped desperately for an opening gambit but came up with nothing. The ticking of the clock boomed out into the silence. I was beginning to break out into a sweat when the little man cleared his throat.

'Pigs were a good trade on Monday,' he vouchsafed.

'They were, eh? Well, that's fine — jolly good.'

Mr Alderson nodded, fixed his gaze somewhere above my left shoulder and started drumming his fingers again. Once more the heavy silence blanketed us and the clock continued to hammer out its message.

After several years Mr Alderson stirred in his seat and gave a little cough. I looked at him eagerly.

'Store cattle were down, though,' he said.

'Ah, too bad, what a pity,' I babbled. 'But that's how it goes, I suppose, eh?'

Helen's father shrugged and we settled down again. This time I knew it was hopeless. My mind was a void and my companion had the defeated look of a man who has shot his conversational bolt. I lay back and studied the hams and sides of bacon hanging from their hooks in the ceiling, then I worked my way along the row of plates on the big oak dresser to a gaudy calendar from a cattle cake firm which dangled from a nail on the wall. I took a chance then and stole a glance at Mr Alderson out of the corner of my eye and my toes curled as I saw he had chosen that precise moment to have a sideways peep at me. We both looked away hurriedly.

By shifting round in my seat and craning my neck I was able to get a view of the other side of the kitchen where there was an old-fashioned roll top desk surmounted by a wartime picture of Mr Alderson looking very stern in the uniform of the Yorkshire Yeomanry, and I was proceeding along the wall from there when Helen opened the door and came quickly into the room.

'Dad,' she said, a little breathlessly. 'Stan's here. He says one of the cows is down with staggers.'

Her father jumped up in obvious relief. I think he was delighted he had a sick cow and I, too, felt like a released prisoner as I hurried out with him.

Stan, one of the cowmen, was waiting in

the yard.

'She's at t'top of t'field, boss,' he said. 'I just spotted 'er when I went to get them in for milkin'.'

Mr Alderson looked at me questioningly and I nodded at him as I opened the car door.

'I've got the stuff with me,' I said. 'We'd better drive straight up.'

The three of us piled in and I set course to where I could see the stretched-out form of a cow near the wall in the top corner. My bottles and instruments rattled and clattered as we bumped over the rig and furrow.

This was something every vet gets used to in early summer; the urgent call to milk cows which have collapsed suddenly a week or two after being turned out to grass. The farmers called it grass staggers and as its scientific name of hypomagesaemia implied it was associated with lowered magnesium level in the blood. An alarming and highly fatal condition but fortunately curable by injection of magnesium in most cases.

Despite the seriousness of the occasion I

couldn't repress a twinge of satisfaction. It had got me out of the house and it gave me a chance to prove myself by doing something useful. Helen's father and I hadn't established anything like a rapport as yet, but maybe when I gave his unconscious cow my magic injection and it leaped to its feet and walked away he might look at me in a different light. And it often happened that way; some of the cures were really dramatic.

'She's still alive, any road,' Stan said as we roared over the grass. 'I saw her legs move then.'

He was right, but as I pulled up and jumped from the car I felt a tingle of apprehension. Those legs were moving too much.

This was the kind that often died; the convulsive type. The animal, prone on her side, was pedalling frantically at the air with all four feet, her head stretched backwards, eyes staring, foam bubbling from her mouth. As I hurriedly unscrewed the cap from the bottle of magnesium lactate she stopped and went into a long, shuddering spasm, legs stiffly extended, eyes screwed tightly shut; then she relaxed and lay inert for a frightening few seconds before recommencing the wild thrashing with her legs.

My mouth had gone dry. This was a bad one. The strain on the heart during these spasms was enormous and each one could be her last.

I crouched by her side, my needle poised over the milk vein. My usual practice was to inject straight into the blood stream to achieve the quickest possible effect, but in this case I hesitated. Any interference with the heart's action could kill this cow; best to play safe — I reached over and pushed the needle under the skin of the neck.

As the fluid ran in, bulging the subcutaneous tissues and starting a widening swelling under the roan-coloured hide, the cow went into another spasm. For an agonising few seconds she lay there, the quivering limbs reaching desperately out at nothing, the eyes disappearing deep down under tight-twisted lids. Helplessly I watched her, my heart thudding, and this time as she came out of the rigor and started to move again it wasn't with the purposeful peddling of before; it was an aimless laboured pawing and as even this grew weaker her eyes slowly opened and gazed outwards with a vacant stare.

I bent and touched the cornea with my finger, there was no response.

The farmer and cowman looked at me in silence as the animal gave a final jerk then lay still.

'I'm afraid she's dead, Mr Alderson,' I said.

The farmer nodded and his eyes moved slowly over the still form, over the graceful limbs, the fine dark roan flanks, the big, turgid udder that would give no more milk.

'I'm sorry,' I said. 'I'm afraid her heart must have given out before the magnesium had a chance to work.'

'It's a bloody shame,' grunted Stan. 'She was a right good cow, that 'un.'

Mr Alderson turned quietly back to the car. 'Aye well, these things happen,' he muttered.

We drove down the field to the house.

Inside, the work was over and the family collected in the parlour. I sat with them for a while but my overriding emotion was an urgent desire to be elsewhere. Helen's father had been silent before but now he sat hunched miserably in an armchair taking no part in the conversation. I wondered whether he thought I had actually killed his cow. It certainly hadn't looked very good, the vet walking up to the sick animal, the quick injection and hey presto, dead. No, I had been blameless but it hadn't looked good.

On an impulse I jumped to my feet.

'Thank you very much for the lovely tea,' I said, 'but I really must be off. I'm on duty this evening.'

Helen came with me to the door. 'Well it's been nice seeing you again, Jim.' She paused and looked at me doubtfully. 'I wish you'd stop worrying about that cow. It's a pity but you couldn't help it. There was nothing you could do.'

'Thanks, Helen, I know. But it's a nasty smack for your father isn't it?'

She shrugged and smiled her kind smile. Helen was always kind.

Driving back through the pastures up to the farm gate I could see the motionless body of my patient with her companions sniffing around her curiously in the gentle evening sunshine. Any time now the knacker man would be along to winch the carcase on to his wagon. It was the grim epilogue to every vet's failure.

I closed the gate behind me and looked back at Heston Grange. I had thought everything would be all right this time but it hadn't worked out that way.

The jinx was still on.

# Chapter 8

'Monday morning disease' they used to call it. The almost unbelievably gross thickening of the hind limb in cart horses which had stood in the stable over the weekend. It seemed that the sudden suspension of their normal work and exercise produced the massive lymphangitis and swelling which gave many a farmer a nasty jolt right at the begining of the week.

But it was Wednesday evening now and Mr Crump's big Shire gelding was greatly improved.

'That leg's less than half the size it was,' I said, running my hand over the inside of the hock, feeling the remains of the oedema pitting under my fingers. 'I can see you've put in some hard work here.'

'Aye, ah did as you said.' Mr Crump's reply was typically laconic, but I knew he must have spent hours fomenting and massaging the limb and forcibly exercising the horse as I had told him when I gave the arecoline injection on Monday.

I began to fill the syringe for a repeat injection. 'He's having no corn, is he?'

'Nay, nowt but bran.'

'That's fine. I think he'll be back to normal in a day or two if you keep up the treatment.'

The farmer grunted and no sign of approval showed in the big, purple-red face with its perpetually surprised expression. But I knew he was pleased all right; he was fond of the horse and had been unable to hide his concern at the animal's pain and distress on my first visit.

I went into the house to wash my hands and Mr Crump led the way into the kitchen, his big frame lumbering clumsily ahead of me. He proferred soap and towel in his slow-moving way and stood back in silence as I leaned over the long shallow sink of brown earthenware.

As I dried my hands he cleared his

throat and spoke hesitantly. 'Would you like a drink of ma wine?'

Before I could answer, Mrs Crump came bustling through from an inner room. She was pulling on her hat and behind her her teen-age son and daughter followed, dressed ready to go out.

'Oh Albert, stop it!' she snapped, looking up at her husband. 'Mr Herriot doesn't want your wine. I wish you wouldn't pester people so with it!'

The boy grinned. 'Dad and his wine, he's always looking for a victim.' His sister joined in the general laughter and I had an uncomfortable feeling that Mr Crump was the odd man out in his own home.

'We're going down t'village institute to see a school play, Mr Herriot,' the wife said briskly. 'We're late now so we must be off.' She hurried away with her children, leaving the big man looking after her sheepishly.

There was a silence while I finished drying my hands, then I turned to the farmer. 'Well, how about that drink, Mr Crump?'

He hesitated for a moment and the surprised look deepened. 'Would you . . . you'd really like to try some?'

'I'd love to. I haven't had my evening meal yet — I could just do with an aperitif.'

'Right, I'll be back in a minute.' He disappeared into the large pantry at the end of the kitchen and came back with a bottle of amber liquid and glasses.

'This is ma rhubarb,' he said, tipping out two good measures.

I took a sip and then a good swallow, and gasped as the liquid blazed a firey trail down to my stomach.

'It's strong stuff,' I said a little breathlessly, 'but the taste is very pleasant. Very pleasant indeed.'

Mr Crump watched approvingly as I took another drink. 'Aye, it's just right. Nearly two years old.'

I drained the glass and this time the wine didn't burn so much on its way down but seemed to wash around the walls of my empty stomach and send glowing tendrils creeping along my limbs.

'Delicious,' I said. 'Absolutely delicious.'

The farmer expanded visibly. He refilled the glasses and watched with rapt attention as I drank. When we had finished the second glass he jumped to his feet.

'Now for a change I want you to try summat different.' He almost trotted to the pantry and produced another bottle, this time of colourless fluid. 'Elderflower,' he said, panting slightly.

When I tasted it I was amazed at the delicate flavour, the bubbles sparkling and dancing on my tongue.

'Gosh, this is terrific! It's just like champagne. You know, you really have a gift — I never thought home made wines could taste like this.'

Mr Crump stared at me for a moment then one corner of his mouth began to twitch and incredibly a shy smile spread slowly over his face. 'You're about fust I've heard say that. You'd think I was trying to poison folks when I offer them ma wine — they always shy off but they can sup plenty of beer and whisky.'

'Well they don't know what they're missing, Mr Crump.' I watched while the farmer replenished my glass. 'I wouldn't have believed you could make stuff as good as this at home.' I sipped appreciatively at the elderflower. It still tasted like champagne.

I hadn't got more than half way down the glass before Mr Crump was clattering and clinking inside the pantry again. He emerged with a bottle with contents of a deep blood red. 'Try that,' he gasped.

I was beginning to feel like a professional taster and rolled the first mouthful around my mouth with eyes half closed. 'Mm, mm, yes. Just like an excellent port, but there's something else here — a fruitiness in the background — something familiar about it — it's. . . it's . . . '

'Blackberry!' shouted Mr Crump triumphantly. 'One of t'best I've done. Made it two back-ends since — it were a right good year for it.'

Leaning back in the chair I took another drink of the rich, dark wine; it was round-flavoured, warming, and behind it there was always the elusive hint of the brambles. I could almost see the heavy-hanging clusters of berries glistening black and succulent in the autumn sunshine. The mellowness of the image matched my mood which was becoming more expansive by the minute and I looked round with leisurely appreciation at the rough comfort of the farmhouse kitchen; at the hams and sides of bacon hanging from their hooks in the ceiling, and at my host sitting across the table, watching me eagerly. He was, I noticed for the first time, still wearing his cap.

'You know,' I said, holding the glass high and studying its ruby depths against the light, 'I can't make up my mind which of your wines I like best. They're all excellent and yet so different.'

Mr Crump, too, had relaxed. He threw back his head and laughed delightedly before hurriedly refilling both of our tumblers. 'But you haven't started yet. Ah've got dozens of bottles in there — all different. You must try a few more.' He shambled again over to the pantry and this time when he reappeared he was weighed down by an armful of bottles of differing shapes and colours.

What a charming man he was, I thought. How wrong I had been in my previous assessment of him; it had been so easy to put him down as lumpish and unemotional but as I looked at him now his face was alight with friendship, hospitality, understanding. He had cast off his inhibitions and as he sat down surrounded by the latest batch he began to talk rapidly and fluently about wines and wine-making.

Wide-eyed and impassioned he ranged at length over the niceties of fermentation and sedimentation, of flavour and bouquet. He dealt learnedly with the relative merits of Chambertin and Nuits St George, Montrachet and Chablis. Enthusiasts are appealing but a fanatic is irresistible and I sat spellbound while Mr Crump pushed endless samples of his craft in front of me, mixing and adjusting expertly.

'How did you find that 'un?'

'Very nice . . .'

'Bit sweet, maybe?'

'Well, perhaps . . .

'Right, try some of this with it.' The meticulous addition of a few drops of nameless liquid from the packed rows of bottles. 'How's that?'

'Marvellous!'

'Now this 'un. Perhaps a bit sharpish, eh?

'Possibly . . . yes . . .'

Again the tender trickling of a few mysterious droplets into my drink and again the anxious enquiry.

'Is that better?'

'Just right.'

The big man drank with me, glass by glass. We tried parsnip and dandelion, cowslip and parsley, clover, gooseberry, beetroot and crab apple. Incredibly we had some stuff made from turnips which was so exquisite that I insisted on a refill.

Everything gradually slowed down as we sat there. Time slowed down till it was finally meaningless. Mr Crump and I slowed down and our speech and actions became more and more deliberate. The farmer's visits to the pantry developed into laboured, unsteady affairs; sometimes he took a roundabout route to reach the door and on one occasion there was a tremendous crash from within and I feared he had fallen among his bottles. But I couldn't be bothered to get up to see and in due course he reappeared, apparently unharmed.

It was around nine o'clock that I heard the soft knocking on the outer door. I ignored it as I didn't want to interrupt Mr Crump who was in the middle of a deep exposition.

'Thish,' he was saying, leaning close to me and tapping a bulbous flagon with his forefinger. 'Thish is, in my 'pinion, comp'rable to a fine Moselle. Made it lash year and would 'preciate it if you'd tell me what you think.' He bent low over the glass, blinking, heavy-eyed as he poured.

'Now then, wha' d'you say? Ish it or ishn't it?'

I took a gulp and paused for a moment. It all tasted the same now and I had never drunk Moselle anyway, but I nodded and hiccuped solemnly in reply.

The farmer rested a friendly hand on my shoulder and was about to make a further speech when he, too, heard the knocking. He made his way across the floor with some difficulty and opened the door. A young lad was standing there and I heard a few muttered words.

'We 'ave a cow on calving and we 'phoned surgery and they said vitnery might still be here.'

Mr Crump turned to face me. 'It's the Bamfords of Holly Bush. They wan' you to go there — jush a mile along t'road.'

'Right,' I heaved myself to my feet then gripped the table tightly as the familiar objects of the room began to whirl rapidly around me. When they came to rest Mr Crump appeared to be standing at the head of a fairly steep slope. The kitchen floor had seemed perfectly level when I had come in but now it was all I could do to fight my way up the gradient.

When I reached the door Mr Crump was staring owlishly into the darkness.

''Sraining,' he said. ''sraining like 'ell.'

I peered out at the steady beat of the dark water on the cobbles of the yard, but my car was just a few yards away and I was about to set out when the farmer caught my arm.

'Jus' minute, can't go out like that.' He held up a finger then went over and groped about in a drawer. At length he produced a tweed cap which he offered me with great dignity.

I never wore anything on my head whatever the weather but I was deeply touched and wrung my companion's hand in silence. It was understandable that a man like Mr Crump who wore his cap at all times, indoors and out, would recoil in horror from the idea of anybody venturing uncovered into the rain.

The tweed cap which I now put on was the biggest I had ever seen; a great round flat pancake of a thing which even at that moment I felt would keep not only my head but my shoulders and entire body dry in the heaviest downpour.

I took my leave of Mr Crump with reluctance and as I settled in the seat of the car trying to remember where first gear was situated I could see his bulky form silhouetted against the light from the kitchen; he was waving his hand with gentle benevolence and it struck me as I at length drove away what a deep and wonderful friendship had been forged that night.

Driving at walking pace along the dark narrow road, my nose almost touching the windscreen, I was conscious of some unusual sensations. My mouth and lips felt abnormally sticky as though I had been drinking liquid glue instead of wine, my breath seemed to be whistling in my nostrils like a strong wind blowing under a door, and I was having difficulty focusing my eyes. Fortunately I met only one car and as it approached and flashed past in the other direction I was muzzily surprised by the fact that it had two complete sets of headlights which kept merging into each other and drawing apart again.

In the yard at Holly Bush I got out of the car, nodded to the shadowy group of figures standing there, fumbled my bottle of antiseptic and calving ropes from the boot and marched determinedly into the byre. One of the men held an oil lamp over a cow lying on a deep bed of straw in one of the standings; from the vulva a calf's foot protruded a few inches and as the cow strained a little muzzle showed momentarily then disappeared as she relaxed.

Far away inside me a stone cold sober veterinary surgeon murmured: 'Only a leg back and a big roomy cow. Shouldn't be much trouble.' I turned and looked at the Bamfords for the first time. I hadn't met them before but it was easy to classify them; simple, kindly, anxious-to-please people — two middle-aged men, probably brothers, and two young men who would be the sons of one or the other. They were all staring at me in the dim light, their eyes expectant, their mouths slightly open as though ready to smile or laugh if given half a chance.

I squared my shoulders, took a deep breath and said in a loud voice: 'Would you please bring me a bucket of hot water, some soap and a towel.' Or at least that's what I meant to say, because what actually issued from my lips was a torrent of something that sounded like Swahili. The Bamfords, poised, ready to spring into action to do my bidding, looked at me blankly. I cleared by throat, swallowed, took a few seconds' rest and tried again. The result was the same — another volley of gibberish echoing uselessly round the cow house.

Clearly I had a problem. It was essential to communicate in some way, particularly since these people didn't know me and were waiting for some action. I suppose I must have appeared a strange and enigmatic figure standing there, straight and solemn, surmounted and dominated by the vast cap. But through the mists a flash of insight showed me where I was going wrong. It was over-confidence. It wasn't a bit of good trying to speak loudly like that. I tried again in the faintest of whispers.

'Could I have a bucket of hot water, some soap and a towel, please.' It came out beautifully though the oldest Mr Bamford didn't quite get it first time. He came close, cupped an ear with his hand and watched my lips intently. Then he nodded eagerly in comprehension, held up a forefinger at me, tiptoed across the floor like a tight rope walker to one of the sons and whispered in his ear. The young man turned and crept out noiselessly, closing the door behind him with the utmost care; he was back in less than a minute, padding over the cobbles daintily in his heavy boots and placing the bucket gingerly in front of me.

I managed to remove my jacket, tie and shirt quite efficiently and they were taken from me in silence and hung up on nails by the Bamfords who were moving around as though in church. I thought I was doing fine till I started to wash my arms. The soap kept shooting from my arms, slithering into the dung channel, disappearing into the dark corners of the byre with the Bamfords in hot pursuit. It was worse still when I tried to work up to the top of my arms. The soap flew over my shoulders like a live thing, at times cannoning off the walls, at others gliding down my back. The farmers never knew where the next shot was going and they took on the appearance of a really sharp fielding side crouching around me with arms outstretched waiting for a catch.

However I did finally work up a lather and was ready to start, but the cow refused firmly to get to her feet, so I had to stretch out behind her face down on the unyielding cobbles. It wasn't till I had got down there that I felt the great cap dropping over my ears; I must have put it on again after removing my shirt though it was difficult to see what purpose it might serve.

Inserting a hand gently into the vagina I pushed along the calf's neck, hoping to come upon a flexed knee or even a foot, but I was disappointed; the leg really was right back, stretching from the shoulder away flat against the calf's side. Still, I would be all right — it just meant a longer reach.

And there was one reassuring feature; the calf was alive. As I lay, my face was almost touching the rear end of the cow and I had a close up of the nose which kept appearing every few seconds; it was good to see the little nostrils twitching as they sought the outside air. All I had to do was get that leg round.

But the snag was that as I reached forward the cow kept straining, squeezing my arm cruelly against her bony pelvis, making me groan and roll about in agony for a few seconds till the pressure went off. Quite often in these crises my cap fell on to the floor and each time gentle hands replaced it immediately on my head.

At last the foot was in my hand — there would be no need for ropes this time — and I began to pull it round. It took me longer than I thought and it seemed to me that the calf was beginning to lose patience with me because when its head was forced out by the cow's contractions we were eye to eye and I fancied the little creature was giving me a disgusted 'For heaven's sake get on with it' look.

When the leg did come round it was with a rush and in an instant everything was laid as it should have been.

'Get hold of the feet,' I whispered to the Bamfords and after a hushed consultation they took up their places. In no time at all a fine heifer calf was wriggling on the cobbles shaking its head and snorting the placental fluid from its nostrils.

In response to my softly hissed instructions the farmers rubbed the little creature down with straw wisps and pulled it round for its mother to lick.

It was a happy ending to the most peaceful calving I have ever attended. Never a voice raised, everybody moving around on tiptoe. I got dressed in a cathedral silence, went out to the car, breathed a final goodnight and left with the Bamfords waving mutely.

To say I had a hangover next morning would be failing even to hint at the utter disintegration of my bodily economy and personality. Only somebody who had consumed two or three quarts of assorted home made wines at a sitting could have an inkling of the quaking nausea, the raging inferno within, the jangling nerves, the black despairing outlook.

Tristan had seen me in the bathroom running the cold tap on my tounge and had intuitively administered a raw egg, aspirins and brandy which, as I came downstairs, lay in a cold, unmoving blob in my outraged stomach.

'What are you walking like that for, James?' asked Siegfried in what sounded like a bull's bellow as I came in on him at breakfast. 'You look as though you'd pee'd yourself.'

'Oh it's nothing much.' It was no good telling him I was treading warily across the carpet because I was convinced that if I let my heels down too suddenly it would jar my eyeballs from their sockets. 'I had a few glasses of Mr Crump's wine last night and it seems to have upset me.'

'A few glasses! You ought to be more careful — that stuff's dynamite. Could knock anybody over.' He crashed his cup into its saucer then began to clatter about with knife and fork as if trying to give a one man rendering of the Anvil Chorus. 'I hope you weren't any the worse to go to the Bamford's.'

I listlessly crumbled some dry toast on my plate. 'Well I did the job all right, but I'd had a bit too much — no use denying it.'

Siegfried was in one of his encouraging moods. 'By God, James, those Bamfords are very strict methodists. They're grand chaps but absolutely dead nuts against drink — if they thought you were under the influence of alcohol they'd never have you on the place again.' He ruthlessly bisected an egg yolk. 'I hope they didn't notice anything. Do you think they knew?'

'Oh maybe not. No, I shouldn't think so.' I closed my eyes and shivered as Siegfried pushed a forkful of sausage and fried bread into his mouth and began to chew briskly. My mind went back to the gentle hands replacing the monstrous cap on my head and I groaned inwardly.

Those Bamfords knew all right. Oh yes, they knew.

# Chapter 9

The silver haired old gentleman with the pleasant face didn't look the type to be easily upset but his eyes glared at me angrily and his lips quivered with indignation.

'Mr Herriot,' he said. 'I have come to make a complaint. I strongly object to your allowing students to practise on my cat.'

'Students? What students?' I was mystified.

'I think you know, Mr Herriot. I brought my cat in a few days ago for a hysterectomy and I am referring to this operation.'

I nodded. 'Yes, I remember it very well . . . but where do the students come in?'

'Well the operation wound was rather large and I have it on good authority that it was made by somebody who was just learning the job.' The old gentleman stuck out his chin fiercely.

'Right,' I said. 'Let's take one thing at a time. I did that operation myself and I had to enlarge the wound because your cat was in an advanced state of pregnancy. I couldn't squeeze the foetuses through my original incision.'

'Oh? I didn't know that.'

'Secondly, we have no students with us. They only come at holiday times and when they are here they certainly are not allowed to carry out operations.'

'Well this lady seemed to be absolutely sure of her facts. She was adamant about it. She took one look at the cat and pronounced that it was the work of a student.'

'Lady?'

'Yes,' said the old gentleman. 'She is very clever with animals and she came round to see if she could help in my cat's convalescence. She brought some excellent condition powders with her.'

'Ah!' A blinding shaft pierced the fog in my mind. All was suddenly clear. 'It was Mrs Donovan, wasn't it?'

'Well . . . er, yes. That was her name.'

Old Mrs Donovan was a woman who really got around. No matter what was going on in Darrowby — weddings, funerals, house-sales — you'd find the dumpy little figure and walnut face among the spectators, the darting, black-button eyes taking everything in. And always, on the end of its lead, her terrier dog.

When I say 'old', I'm only guessing, because she appeared ageless; she seemed to have been around a long time but she could have been anything between fifty five and seventy five. She certainly had the vitality of a young woman because she must have walked vast distances in her dedicated quest to keep abreast of events. Many people took an uncharitable view of her acute curiosity but whatever the motivation, her activities took her into almost every channel of life in the town. One of these channels was our veterinary practice.

Because Mrs Donovan, among her other widely ranging interests, was an animal doctor. In fact I think it would be safe to say that this facet of her life transcended all the others.

She could talk at length on the ailments of small animals and she had a whole armoury of medicines and remedies at her command, her two specialities being her miracle working condition powders and a dog shampoo of unprecedented value for improving the coat. She had an uncanny ability to sniff out a sick animal and it was not uncommon when I was on my rounds to find Mrs Donovan's dark gipsy face poised intently over what I had thought was my patient while she administered calf's foot jelly or one of her own patent nostrums.

I suffered more than Siegfried because I took a more active part in the small animal side of our practice. I was anxious to develop this aspect and to improve my image in this field and Mrs Donovan didn't help at all. 'Young Mr Herriot,' she would confide to my clients, 'is all right with cattle and such like, but he don't know nothing about dogs and cats.

And of course they believed her and had implicit faith in her. She had the irresistible mystic appeal of the amateur and on top of that there was her habit, particularly endearing in Darrowby, of never charging for her advice, her medicines, her long periods of diligent nursing.

Older folk in the town told how her husband, an Irish farm worker, had died many years ago and how he must have had a 'bit put away' because Mrs Donovan had apparently been able to indulge all her interests over the years without financial strain. Since she inhabited the streets of Darrowby all day and every day I often encountered her and she always smiled up at me sweetly and told me how she had been sitting up all night with Mrs So-and-so's dog that I'd been treating. She felt sure she'd be able to pull it through.

There was no smile on her face, however, on the day when she rushed into the surgery while Siegfried and I were having tea.

'Mr Herriot!' she gasped. 'Can you come? My little dog's been run over!'

I jumped up and ran out to the car with her. She sat in the passenger seat with her head bowed, her hands clasped tightly on her knees.

'He slipped his collar and ran in front of a car,' she murmured. 'He's lying in front of the school half way up Cliffend Road. Please hurry.'

I was there within three minutes but as I bent over the dusty little body stretched on the pavement I knew there was nothing I could do. The fast-glazing eyes, the faint, gasping respirations, the ghastly pallor of the mucous membranes all told the same story.

'I'll take him back to the surgery and get some saline into him, Mrs Donovan,' I said. 'But I'm afraid he's had a massive internal haemorrhage. Did you see what happened exactly?'

She gulped. 'Yes, the wheel went right over him.'

Ruptured liver, for sure. I passed my hands under the little animal and began to lift him gently, but as I did so the breathing stopped and the eyes stared fixedly ahead.

Mrs Donovan sank to her knees and for a few moments she gently stroked the rough hair of the head and chest. 'He's dead, isn't he?' she whispered at last.

'I'm afraid he is,' I said.

She got slowly to her feet and stood bewilderedly among the little group of bystanders on the pavement. Her lips moved but she seemed unable to say any more.

I took her arm, led her over to the car and opened the door. 'Get in and sit down,' I said. 'I'll run you home. Leave everything to me.'

I wrapped the dog in my calving overall and laid him in the boot before driving away. It wasn't until we drew up outside Mrs Donovan's house that she began to weep silently. I sat there without speaking till she had finished. Then she wiped her eyes and turned to me.

'Do you think he suffered at all?'

'I'm certain he didn't. It was all so quick — he wouldn't know a thing about it.'

She tried to smile. 'Poor little Rex, I don't know what I'm going to do without him. We've travelled a few miles together, you know.'

'Yes, you have. He had a wonderful life, Mrs Donovan. And let me give you a bit of advice — you must get another dog. You'd be lost without one.'

She shook her head. 'No, I couldn't. That little dog meant too much to me. I couldn't let another take his place.'

'Well I know that's how you feel just now but I wish you'd think about it. I don't want to seem callous — I tell everybody this when they lose an animal and I know it's good advice.'

'Mr Herriot, I'll never have another one.' She shook her head again, very decisively. 'Rex was my faithful friend for many years and I just want to remember him. He's the last dog I'll ever have.'

I often saw Mrs Donovan around the town after this and I was glad to see she was still as active as ever, though she looked strangely incomplete without the little dog on its lead. But it must have been over a month before I had the chance to speak to her.

It was on the afternoon that Inspector

Halliday of the R.S.P.C.A. rang me.

'Mr Herriot,' he said, 'I'd like you to come and see an animal with me. A cruelty case.'

'Right, what is it?'

'A dog, and it's pretty grim. A dreadful case of neglect.' He gave me the name of a row of old brick cottages down by the river and said he'd meet me there.

Halliday was waiting for me, smart and business-like in his dark uniform, as I pulled up in the back lane behind the houses. He was a big, blond man with cheerful blue eyes but he didn't smile as he came over to the car.

'He's in here.' he said, and led the way towards one of the doors in the long, crumbling wall. A few curious people were hanging around and with a feeling of inevitability I recognised a gnome-like brown face. Trust Mrs Donovan, I thought, to be among those present at a time like this.

We went through the door into the long garden. I had found that even the lowliest dwellings in Darrowby had long strips of land at the back as though the builders had taken it for granted that the country people who were going to live in them would want to occupy themselves with the pursuits of the soil; with vegetable and fruit growing, even stock keeping in a small way. You usually found a pig there, a few hens, often pretty beds of flowers.

But this garden was a wilderness. A chilling air of desolation hung over the few gnarled apple and plum trees standing among a tangle of rank grass as though the place had been forsaken by all living creatures.

Halliday went over to a ramshackle wooden shed with peeling paint and a rusted corrugated iron roof. He produced a key, unlocked the padlock and dragged the door partly open. There was no window and it wasn't easy to identify the jumble inside; broken gardening tools, an ancient mangle, rows of flower pots and partly used paint tins. And right at the back, a dog sitting quietly.

I didn't notice him immediately because of the gloom and because the smell in the shed started me coughing, but as I drew closer I saw that he was a big animal, sitting very upright, his collar secured by a chain to a ring in the wall. I had seen some thin dogs but this advanced emaciation reminded me of my text books on anatomy; nowhere else did the bones of pelvis, face and rib cage stand out with such horrifying clarity. A deep, smoothed out hollow in the earth floor showed where he had lain, moved about, in fact lived for a very long time.

The sight of the animal had a stupefying effect on me; I only half took in the rest of the scene — the filthy shreds of sacking scattered nearby, the bowl of scummy water.

'Look at his back end,' Halliday muttered.

I carefully raised the dog from his sitting position and realised that the stench in the place was not entirely due to the piles of excrement. The hind-quarters were a welter of pressure sores which had turned gangrenous and strips of sloughing tissue hung down from them. There were similar sores along the sternum and ribs. The coat, which seemed to be a dull yellow, was matted and caked with dirt.

The Inspector spoke again. 'I don't think he's ever been out of here. He's only a young dog — about a year old — but I understand he's been in this shed since he was an eight week old pup. Somebody out in the lane heard a whimper or he'd never have been found.'

I felt a tightening of the throat and a sudden nausea which wasn't due to the smell. It was the thought of this patient animal sitting starved and forgotten in the darkness and filth for a year. I looked again at the dog and saw in his eyes only a calm trust. Some dogs would have barked their heads off and soon been discovered, some would have become terrified and vicious, but this was one of the totally undemanding kind, the kind which had complete faith in people and accepted all their actions without complaint. Just an occasional whimper perhaps as he sat interminably in the empty blackness which had been his world and at times wondered what it was all about.

'Well, Inspector, I hope you're going to throw the book at whoever's responsible,' I said.

Halliday grunted. 'Oh, there won't be much done. It's a case of diminished responsibility. The owner's definitely simple. Lives with an aged mother who hardly knows what's going on either. I've seen the fellow and it seems he threw in a bit of food when he felt like it and that's about all he did. They'll fine him and stop him keeping an animal in the future but nothing more than that.'

'I see.' I reached out and stroked the dog's head and he immediately responded by resting a paw on my wrist. There was a pathetic dignity about the way he held himself erect, the calm eyes regarding me, friendly and unafraid. 'Well, you'll let me know if you want me in court.'

'Of course, and thank you for coming along.' Halliday hesitated for a moment. 'And now I expect you'll want to put this poor thing out of his misery right away.'

I continued to run my hand over the head and ears while I thought for a moment. 'Yes . . . yes, I suppose so. We'd never find a home for him in this state. It's the kindest thing to do. Anyway, push the door wide open will you so that I can get a proper look at him.'

In the improved light I examined him more thoroughly. Perfect teeth, well-proportioned limbs with a fringe of yellow hair. I put my stethoscope on his chest and as I listened to the slow, strong thudding of the heart the dog again put his paw on my hand.

I turned to Halliday. 'You know, Inspector, inside this bag of bones there's a lovely healthy Golden Retriever. I wish there was some way of letting him out.'

As I spoke I noticed there was more than one figure in the door opening. A pair of black pebble eyes were peering intently at the dog from behind the Inspector's broad back. The other spectators had remained in the lane but Mrs Donovan's curiosity had been too much for her. I continued conversationally as though I hadn't seen her.

'You know, what this dog needs first of all is a good shampoo to clean up his matted coat.'

'Huh?' said Halliday.

'Yes. And then he wants a long course of some really strong condition powders.'

154

'What's that?' The Inspector looked startled.

'There's no doubt about it,' I said. 'It's the only hope for him, but where are you going to find such things? Really powerful enough, I mean.' I sighed and straightened up. 'Ah well, I suppose there's nothing else for it. I'd better put him to sleep right away. I'll get the things from my car.'

When I got back to the shed Mrs Donovan was already inside examining the dog despite the feeble remonstrances of the big man.

'Look!' she said excitedly, pointing to a name roughly scratched on the collar. 'His name's Roy.' She smiled up at me. 'It's a bit like Rex, isn't it, that name.'

'You know, Mrs Donovan, now you mention it, it is. It's very like Rex, the way it comes off your tongue.' I nodded seriously.

She stood silent for a few moments, obviously in the grip of a deep emotion, then she burst out.

'Can I have 'im? I can make him better, I know I can. Please, please let me

155

have 'im!'

'Well I don't know,' I said. 'It's really up to the Inspector. You'll have to get his permission.'

Halliday looked at her in bewilderment, then said: 'Excuse me, Madam,' and drew me to one side. We walked a few yards through the long grass and stopped under a tree.

'Mr Herriot,' he whispered, 'I don't know what's going on here, but I can't just pass over an animal in this condition to anybody who has a casual whim. The poor beggar's had one bad break already — I think it's enough. This woman doesn't look a suitable person . . .'

I held up a hand. 'Believe me, Inspector, you've nothing to worry about. She's a funny old stick but she's been sent from heaven today. If anybody in Darrowby can give this dog a new life it's her.'

Halliday still looked very doubtful. 'But I still don't get it. What was all that stuff about him needing shampoos and condition powders?'

'Oh never mind about that. I'll tell you

some other time. What he needs is lots of good grub, care and affection and that's just what he'll get. You can take my word for it.'

'All right, you seem very sure.' Halliday looked at me for a second or two then turned and walked over to the eager little figure by the shed.

I had never before been deliberately on the look out for Mrs Donovan: she had just cropped up wherever I happened to be, but now I scanned the streets of Darrowby anxiously day by day without sighting her. I didn't like it when Gobber Newhouse got drunk and drove his bicycle determinedly through a barrier into a ten foot hole where they were laying a new sewer and Mrs Donovan was not in evidence among the happy crowd who watched the council workmen and two policemen trying to get him out; and when she was nowhere to be seen when they had to fetch the fire engine to the fish and chip shop the night the fat burst into flames, I became seriously worried.

Maybe I should have called round to see

how she was getting on with that dog. Certainly I had trimmed off the necrotic tissue and dressed the sores before she took him away, but perhaps he needed something more than that. And yet at the time I had felt a strong conviction that the main thing was to get him out of there and clean him and feed him and nature would do the rest. And I had a lot of faith in Mrs Donovan — far more than she had in me — when it came to animal doctoring; it was hard to believe I'd been completely wrong.

It must have been nearly three weeks and I was on the point of calling at her home when I noticed her stumping briskly along the far side of the market place, peering closely into every shop window exactly as before. The only difference was that she had a big yellow dog on the end of the lead.

I turned the wheel and sent my car bumping over the cobbles till I was abreast of her. When she saw me getting out she stopped and smiled impishly but she didn't speak as I bent over Roy and examined him. He was still a skinny dog but he looked bright and happy, his wounds were healthy and granulating and there was not a speck of dirt in his coat or on his skin. I knew then what Mrs Donovan had been doing all this time; she had been washing and combing and teasing at that filthy tangle till she had finally conquered it.

As I straightened up she seized my wrist in a grip of surprising strength and looked up into my eyes.

'Now Mr Herriot,' she said. 'Haven't I made a difference to this dog!'

'You've done wonders, Mrs Donovan.' I said. 'And you've been at him with that marvellous shampoo of yours, haven't you?'

She giggled and walked away and from that day I saw the two of them frequently but at a distance and something like two months went by before I had a chance to talk to her again. She was passing by the surgery as I was coming down the steps and again she grabbed my wrist.

'Mr. Herriot,' she said, just as she had done before. 'Haven't I made a difference to this dog!'

I looked down at Roy with something akin to awe. He had grown and filled out and his coat, no longer yellow but a rich gold, lay in luxuriant shining swathes over the well-fleshed ribs and back. A new, brightly studded collar glittered on his neck and his tail, beautifully fringed, fanned the air gently. He was now a Golden Retriever in full magnificence. As I stared at him he reared up, plunked his fore paws on my chest and looked into my face, and in his eyes I read plainly the same calm affection and trust I had seen back in that black, noisome shed.

'Mrs. Donovan,' I said softly, 'he's the most beautiful dog in Yorkshire.' Then, because I knew she was waiting for it. 'It's those wonderful condition powders. Whatever do you put in them?'

'Ah, wouldn't you like to know!' She bridled and smiled up at me coquettishly and indeed she was nearer being kissed at that moment than for many years.

I suppose you could say that that was the start of Roy's second life. And as the years passed I often pondered on the beneficent providence which had decreed that an animal which had spent his first twelve months abandoned and unwanted, staring uncomprehendingly into that unchanging, stinking darkness, should be whisked in a moment into an existence of light and movement and love. Because I don't think any dog had it quite so good as Roy from then on.

His diet changed dramatically from odd bread crusts to best stewing steak and biscuit, meaty bones and a bowl of warm milk every evening. And he never missed a thing. Garden fetes, school sports, evictions, gymkhanas — he'd be there. I was pleased to note that as time went on Mrs Donovan seemed to be clocking up an even greater daily mileage. Her expenditure on shoe leather must have been phenomenal, but of course it was absolute pie for Roy — a busy round in the morning, home for a meal then straight out again; it was all go.

Mrs Donovan didn't confine her activities to the town centre; there was a big stretch of common land down by the river where there were seats, and people used to take their dogs for a gallop and she liked to get down there fairly regularly to check on the latest developments on the domestic scene. I often saw Roy loping majestically over the grass among a pack of assorted canines, and when he wasn't doing that he was submitting to being stroked or patted or generally fussed over. He was handsome and he just liked people; it made him irresistible.

It was common knowledge that his mistress had bought a whole selection of brushes and combs of various sizes with which she laboured over his coat. Some people said she had a little brush for his teeth, too, and it might have been true, but he certainly wouldn't need his nails clipped — his life on the roads would keep them down.

Mrs Donovan, too, had her reward; she had a faithful companion by her side every hour of the day and night. But there was more to it than that; she had always had the compulsion to help and heal animals and the salvation of Roy was the high point of her life — a blazing triumph which never dimmed.

I know the memory of it was always fresh because many years later I was sitting on the sidelines at a cricket match and I saw the two of them; the old lady glancing keenly around her, Roy gazing placidly out at the field of play, apparently enjoying every ball. At the end of the match I watched them move away with the dispersing crowd; Roy would be about twelve then and heaven only knows how old Mrs Donovan must have been, but the big golden animal was trotting along effortlessly and his mistress, a little more bent, perhaps, and her head rather nearer the ground, was going very well.

When she saw me she came over and I felt the familiar tight grip on my wrist.

'Mr Herriot,' she said, and in the ark probing eyes the pride was still as warm, the triumph still as bursting new as if it had all happened yesterday.

'Mr Herriot, haven't I made a difference to this dog!'

# Chapter 10

The thing that had changed everything was the tranquil basis of my home life. The vagaries of practice went on and would always go on but behind it all Helen's presence was a warm infinity, a measureless peace. When I looked back at the time before she was my wife it was an uncertain world and events like the Darrowby Show seemed an eternity ago.

I remembered when Siegfried first asked me about it.

'How would you like to officiate at Darrowby Show, James?' He threw the letter he had been reading on to the desk and turned to me.

'I don't mind, but I thought you always did it.'

'I do, but it says in that letter that they've changed the date this year and it happens I'm going to be away that weekend.'

'Oh well, fine. What do I have to do?'

Siegfried ran his eye down his list of calls. 'It's a sinecure, really. More a pleasant day out than anything else. You have to measure the ponies and be on call in case any animals are injured. That's about all. Oh and they want you to judge the Family Pets.'

'Family Pets?'

'Yes, they run a proper dog show but they have an expert judge for that. This is just a bit of fun — all kinds of pets. You've got to find a first, second and third.'

'Right,' I said. 'I think I should just about be able to manage that.'

'Splendid.' Siegfried tipped up the envelope in which the letter had come. 'Here are your car park and luncheon tickets for self and friend if you want to take somebody with you. Also your vet's badge. O.K.?'

The Saturday of the show brought the kind of weather that must have had the organisers purring with pleasure; a sky of wide, unsullied blue, hardly a whiff of wind and the kind of torrid, brazen sunshine you don't often find in North Yorkshire.

As I drove down towards the show ground I felt I was looking at a living breathing piece of old England; the group of tents and marquees vivid against the green of the riverside field, the women and children in their bright summer dresses, the cattle with their smocked attendants, a line of massive Shire horses parading in the ring.

I parked the car and made for the stewards' tent with its flag hanging limply from the mast. Tristan parted from me there. With the impecunious student's unerring eye for a little free food and entertainment he had taken up my spare tickets. He headed purposefully for the beer tent as I went in to report to the show secretary.

Leaving my measuring stick there I looked around for a while.

A country show is a lot of different things to a lot of different people. Riding horses of all kinds from small ponies to hunters were being galloped up and down and in one ring the judges hovered around a group of mares and their beautiful little foals.

In a corner four men armed with buckets and brushes were washing and grooming a row of young bulls with great concentration, twiddling and crimping the fuzz over the rumps like society hairdressers.

Wandering through the marquees I examined the bewildering variety of produce from stalks of rhubarb to bunches of onions, the flower displays, embroidery, jams, cakes, pies. And the children's section; a painting of 'The Beach at Scarborough' by Annie Heseltine, aged nine; rows of wobbling copperplate handwriting — 'A thing of beauty is a joy for ever' Bernard Peacock, aged twelve.

Drawn by the occasional gusts of melody I strolled across the grass to where the Darrowby and Houlton Silver Band was rendering Poet and Peasant. The bandsmen were of all ages from seventies down to one or two boys of about fourteen and most of them had doffed their uniform tunics as they sweated in the hot sun. Pint pots reposed under many of the chairs and the musicians refreshed themselves frequently with leisurely swigs.

I was particularly fascinated by the conductor, a tiny frail man who looked about eighty. He alone had retained his full uniform, cap and all, and he stood apparently motionless in front of the crescent of bandsmen, chin sunk on chest, arms hanging limply by his sides. It wasn't until I came right up to him that I realised his fingers were twitching in time with the music and that he was, in fact, conducting. And the more I watched him the more fitting it seemed that he should do it like that. The Yorkshireman's loathing of exhibitionism or indeed any outward show of emotion made it unthinkable that he should throw his arms about in the orthodox manner; no doubt he had spent weary hours rehearsing and coaching his players but here, when the results of his labours were displayed to the public, he wasn't going to swank about it. Even the almost imperceptible twitching of the finger-ends had something guilty about it as if the old man felt he was being caught out in something shameful.

But my attention was jerked away as a group of people walked across on the far side of the band. It was Helen with Richard Edmundson and behind them Mr Alderson and Richard's father deep in conversation. The young man walked very close to Helen, his shining, plastered-down fair hair hovering possessively over her dark head, his face animated as he talked and laughed.

There were no clouds in the sky but it was as if a dark hand had reached across and smudged away the brightness of the sunshine. I turned quickly and went in search of Tristan.

I soon picked out my colleague as I hurried into the marquee with 'Refreshments' over the entrance. He was leaning with an elbow on the makeshift counter of boards and trestles chatting contentedly with a knot of cloth-capped locals, a Woodbine in one hand, a pint glass in the other. There was a general air of earthy bonhomie. Drinking of a more decorous kind would be taking place at the president's bar behind the stewards' headquarters with pink gins or sherry as the main tipple but here it was beer, bottled and draught, and the stout ladies behind the counter were working with the fierce concentration of people who knew they were in for a hard day.

'Yes, I saw her,' Tristan said when I gave him my news. 'In fact there she is now.' He nodded in the direction of the family group as they strolled past the entrance. 'I've had my eye on them for some time — I don't miss much from in here you know, Jim.'

'Ah well.' I accepted a half of bitter from him. 'It all looks pretty cosy. The two dads like blood brothers and Helen hanging on to that bloke's arm.'

Tristan squinted over the top of his pint at the scene outside and shook his head. 'Not exactly. He's hanging on to HER arm.' He looked at me judicially. 'There's a difference, you know.'

'I don't suppose it makes much difference to me either way,' I grunted.

'Well don't look so bloody mournful.' He

took an effortless swallow which lowered the level of his glass by about six inches. 'What do you expect an attractive girl to do? Sit at home waiting for you to call? If you've been pounding on her door every night you haven't told me about it.'

'It's all right you talking. I think old man Alderson would set his dogs on me if I showed up there. I know he doesn't like me hanging around Helen and on top of that I've got the feeling he thinks I killed his cow on my last visit.'

'And did you?'

'No, I didn't. But I walked up to a living animal, gave it an injection and it promptly died, so I can't blame him.'

I took a sip at my beer and watched the Alderson party who had changed direction and were heading away from our retreat. Helen was wearing a pale blue dress and I was thinking how well the colour went with the deep brown of her hair and how I liked the way she walked with her legs swinging easily and her shoulders high and straight when the loudspeaker boomed across the show ground.

'Will Mr Herriot, Veterinary Surgeon, please report to the stewards immediately.'

It made me jump but at the same time I felt a quick stab of pride. It was the first time I had heard myself and my profession publicly proclaimed. I turned to Tristan. He was supposed to be seeing practice and this could be something interesting. But he was immersed in a story which he was trying to tell to a little stocky man with a fat, shiny face, and he was having difficulty because the little man, determined to get his full measure of enjoyment, kept throwing himself into helpless convulsions at the end of every sentence, and the finish was a long way away. Tristan took his stories very seriously; I decided not to interrupt him.

A glow of importance filled me as I hurried over the grass, my official badge with 'Veterinary Surgeon' in gold letters dangling from my lapel. A steward met me on the way.

'It's one of the cattle. Had an accident, I think.' He pointed to a row of pens along

172

the edge of the field.

A curious crowd had collected around my patient which had been entered in the in-calf heifers class. The owner a stranger from outside the Darrowby practice came up to me, his face glum.

'She tripped coming off the cattle wagon and went 'ead first into the wall. Knocked one of 'er horns clean off.'

The heifer, a bonny little light roan, was a pathetic sight. She had been washed, combed, powdered and primped for the big day and there she was with one horn dangling drunkenly down the side of her face and an ornamental fountain of bright arterial blood climbing gracefully in three jets from the broken surface high into the air.

I opened my bag. I had brought a selection of the things I might need and I fished out some artery forceps and suture material. The rational way to stop haemorrhage of this type is to grasp the bleeding vessel and ligate it, but it wasn't always as easy as that. Especially when the patient won't cooperate.

The broken horn was connected to the

head only by a band of skin and I quickly snipped it away with scissors; then, with the farmer holding the heifer's nose I began to probe with my forceps for the severed vessels. In the bright sunshine it was surprisingly difficult to see the spurting blood and as the little animal threw her head about I repeatedly felt the warm spray across my face and heard it spatter on my collar.

It was when I was beginning to lose heart with my ineffectual groping that I looked up and saw Helen and her boy friend watching me from the crowd. Young Edmundson looked mildly amused as he watched my unavailing efforts but Helen smiled encouragingly as she caught my eye. I did my best to smile back at her through my bloody mask but I don't suppose it showed.

I gave it up when the heifer gave a particularly brisk toss which sent my forceps flying on to the grass. I did what I should probably have done at the beginning — clapped a pad of cotton wool and antiseptic powder on to the stump and secured it with a figure of eight bandage round the other horn.

'That's it, then,' I said to the farmer as I tried to blink the blood out of my eyes. 'The bleeding's stopped, anyway. I'd advise you to have her properly de-horned soon or she's going to look a bit odd.'

Just then Tristan appeared from among the spectators.

'What's got you out of the beer tent?' I enquired with a touch of bitterness.

'It's lunch time, old lad,' Tristan replied equably. 'But we'll have to get you cleaned up a bit first. I can't be seen with you in that condition. Hang on, I'll get a bucket of water.'

The show luncheon was so excellent that it greatly restored me. Although it was taken in a marquee the committee men's wives had somehow managed to conjure up a memorable cold spread. There was fresh salmon and home fed ham and slices of prime beef with mixed salads and apple pie and the big brimming jugs of cream you only see at farming functions. One of the ladies was a noted cheese maker and we finished with some delicious goat cheese and coffee. The liquid side was catered for too with a bottle of Magnet Pale Ale and a glass at every place.

I didn't have the pleasure of Tristan's company at lunch because he had strategically placed himself well down the table between two strict methodists so that his intake of Magnet was trebled.

I had hardly emerged into the sunshine when a man touched me on the shoulder.

'One of the dog show judges wants you to examine a dog. He doesn't like the look of it.'

He led me to where a thin man of about forty with a small dark moustache was standing by his car. He held a wire-haired fox terrier on a leash and he met me with an ingratiating smile.

'There's nothing whatever the matter with my dog,' he declared, 'but the chap in there seems very fussy.'

I looked down at the terrier. 'I see he has some matter in the corner of his eyes.'

The man shook his head vigorously. 'Oh no, that's not matter. I've been using some white powder on him and a bit's got into his eyes, that's all.'

'Hmm, well let's see what his temperature says, shall we?'

The little animal stood uncomplaining as I inserted the thermometer. When I took the reading my eyebrows went up.

'It's a hundred and four. I'm afraid he's not fit to go into the show.'

'Wait a minute.' The man thrust out his jaw. 'You're talking like that chap in there. I've come a long way to show this dog and I'm going to show him.'

'I'm sorry but you can't show him with a temperature of a hundred and four.'

'But he's had a car journey. That could put up his temperature.'

I shook my head. 'Not as high as that it couldn't. Anyway he looks sick to me. Do you see how he's half closing his eyes as though he's frightened of the light? It's possible he could have distemper.'

'What? That's rubbish and you know it. He's never been fitter!' The man's mouth trembled with anger.

I looked down at the little dog. He was crouching on the grass miserably. Occasionally he shivered, he had a definite photophobia and there was that creamy blob of pus in the corner of each eye. 'Has he been inoculated against distemper?'

'Well no, he hasn't, but why do you keep on about it?'

'Because I think he's got it now and for his sake and for the sake of the other dogs here you ought to take him straight home and see your own vet.'

He glared at me. 'So you won't let me take him into the show tent?'

'That's right. I'm very sorry, but it's out of the question.' I turned and walked away.

I had gone only a few yards when the loudspeaker boomed again. 'Will Mr Herriot please go to the measuring stand where the ponies are ready for him.'

I collected my stick and trotted over to a corner of the field where a group of ponies had assembled; Welsh, Dales, Exmoor, Dartmoor — all kinds of breeds were represented.

For the uninitiated, horses are measured in hands which consist of four inches and a graduated stick is used with a cross piece and a spirit level which rests on the withers, the highest point of the shoulders. I had done a fair bit of it in individual animals but this was the first time I had done the job at a show. With my stick at the ready I stood by the two wide boards which had been placed on the turf to give the animals a reasonably level standing surface.

A smiling young woman led the first pony, a smart chestnut, on to the boards.

'Which class?' I asked.

'Thirteen hands.'

I tried the stick on him. He was well under.

'Fine, next please.'

A few more came through without incident then there was a lull before the next group came up. The ponies were arriving on the field all the time in their boxes and being led over to me, some by their young riders, others by the parents. It looked as though I could be here quite a long time.

During one of the lulls a little man who had been standing near me spoke up.

'No trouble yet?' he asked.

'No, everything's in order,' I replied.

He nodded expressionlessly and as I took a closer look at him his slight body, dark, leathery features and high shoulders seemed to give him the appearance of a little brown gnome. At the same time there was something undeniably horsy about him.

'You'll 'ave some awkward 'uns,' he grunted. 'And they allus say the same thing. They allus tell you the vet at some other show passed their pony.' His swarthy cheeks crinkled in a wry smile.

'Is that so?'

'Aye, you'll see.'

Another candidate, led by a beautiful blonde, was led on to the platform. She gave me the full blast of two big greenish eyes and flashed a mouthful of sparkling teeth at me.

'Twelve two,' she murmured seductively.

I tried the stick on the pony and worked it around, but try as I might I couldn't get it down to that.

'I'm afraid he's a bit big,' I said.

The blonde's smile vanished. 'Have you

allowed half an inch for his shoes?'

'I have indeed, but you can see for yourself, he's well over.'

'But he passed the vet without any trouble at Hickley,' she snapped and out of the corner of my eye I saw the gnome nodding sagely.

'I can't help that,' I said. 'I'm afraid you'll have to put him into the next class.'

For a moment two green pebbles from the cold sea bed fixed me with a frigid glare then the blonde was gone taking her pony with her.

Next, a little bay animal was led on to the stand by a hard faced gentleman in a check suit and I must say I was baffled by its behaviour. Whenever the stick touched the withers it sank at the knees so that I couldn't be sure whether I was getting the right reading or not. Finally I gave up and passed him through.

The gnome coughed. 'I know that feller.'

'You do?'

'Aye, he's pricked that pony's withers with a pin so many times that it drops down whenever you try to measure 'im.'

'Never!'

'Sure as I'm standing here.'

I was staggered, but the arrival of another batch took up my attention for a few minutes. Some I passed, others I had to banish to another class and the owners took it in different ways — some philosophically, a few with obvious annoyance. One or two of the ponies just didn't like the look of the stick at all and I had to dance around them as they backed away and reared.

The last pony in this group was a nice grey led by a bouncy man wearing a great big matey smile.

'How are you, all right?' he inquired courteously. 'This 'un's thirteen two.'

The animal went under the stick without trouble but after he had trotted away the gnome spoke up again.

'I know that feller, too.'

'Really?'

'Not 'alf. Weighs down 'is ponies before they're measured. That grey's been standing in 'is box for the last hour with a twelve stone sack of corn on 'is back. Knocks an inch off.'

'Good God! Are you sure?'

'Don't worry, I've seen 'im at it.'

My mind was beginning to reel just a little. Was the man making it all up or were there really those malign forces at work behind all this innocent fun?

'That same feller,' continued the gnome. 'I've seen 'im bring a pony to a show and get half an inch knocked off for shoes when it never 'ad no shoes on.'

I wished he'd stop. And just then there was an interruption. It was the man with the moustache. He sidled up to me and whispered confidentially in my ear.

'Now I've just been thinking. My dog must have got over his journey by now and I expect his temperature will be normal. I wonder if you'd just try him again. I've still got time to show him.'

I turned wearily. 'Honestly, it'll be a waste of time. I've told you, he's ill.'

'Please! Just as a favour.' He had a desperate look and a fanatical light flickered in his eye.

'All right.' I went over to the car with him and produced my thermometer. The temperature was still a hundred and four.

'Now I wish you'd take this poor little dog home,' I said. 'He shouldn't be here.'

For a moment I thought the man was going to strike me. 'There's nothing wrong with him!' he hissed, his whole face working with emotion.

'I'm sorry,' I said, and went back to the measuring stand.

A boy of about fifteen was waiting for me with his pony. It was supposed to be in the thirteen two class but was nearly one and a half inches over.

'Much too big, I'm afraid,' I said. 'He can't go in that class.'

The boy didn't answer. He put his hand inside his jacket and produced a sheet of paper. 'This is a veterinary certificate to say he's under thirteen two.'

'No good, I'm sorry,' I replied. 'The stewards have told me not to accept any certificates. I've turned down other two today. Everything has to go under the stick. It's a pity, but there it is.'

His manner changed abruptly. 'But you've GOT to accept it!' he shouted in my face. 'There doesn't have to be any measurements when you have a certificate.'

'You'd better see the stewards. Those are my instructions.'

'I'll see my father about this, that's what!' he shouted and led the animal away.

Father was quickly on the scene. Big, fat, prosperous-looking, confident. He obviously wasn't going to stand any nonsense from me.

'Now look here, I don't know what this is all about but you have no option in this matter. You have to accept the certificate.'

'I don't, I assure you,' I answered. 'And anyway, it's not as though your pony was slightly over the mark. He's miles over — nowhere near the height.'

Father flushed dark red. 'Well let me tell you he was passed through by the vet at . . .'

'I know, I know,' I said, and I heard the gnome give a short laugh. 'But he's not going through here.'

There was a brief silence then both father and son began to scream at me. And as they continued to hurl abuse I felt a hand on my arm. It was the man with the moustache again.

'I'm going to ask you just once more to take my dog's temperature,' he whispered with a ghastly attempt at a smile. 'I'm sure he'll be all right this time. Will you try him again?'

I'd had enough. 'No, I bloody well won't!' I barked. 'Will you kindly stop bothering me and take that poor animal home.'

It's funny how the most unlikely things motivate certain people. It didn't seem a life and death matter whether a dog got into a show or not but it was to the man with the moustache. He started to rave at me.

'You don't know your job, that's the trouble with you! I've come all this way and you've played a dirty trick on me. I've got a friend who's a vet, a proper vet, and I'm going to tell him about you, yes I am. I'm going to tell him about you!'

At the same time the father and son were still in full cry, snarling and mouthing at me and I became suddenly aware that I was in the centre of a hostile circle. The blonde was there too, and some of the others whose ponies I had outed and they were all staring at me belligerently, making angry gestures.

I felt very much alone because the gnome, who had seemed an ally, was nowhere to be seen. I was disappointed in the gnome; he was a big talker but had vanished at the first whiff of danger. As I surveyed the threatening crowd I moved my measuring stick round in front of me; it wasn't much of a weapon but it might serve to fend them off if they rushed me.

And just at that moment, as the unkind words were thick upon the air, I saw Helen and Richard Edmundson on the fringe of the circle, taking it all in. I wasn't worried about him but again it struck me as strange that it should be my destiny always to be looking a bit of a clown when Helen was around.

Anyway, the measuring was over and I felt in need of sustenance. I retreated and went to find Tristan.

# Chapter 11

The atmosphere in the beer tent was just what I needed. The hot weather had made the place even more popular than usual and it was crowded; many of the inhabitants had been there since early morning and the air was thick with earthy witticisms, immoderate laughter, cries of joy; and the nice thing was that nobody in there cared a damn about the heights of ponies or the temperatures of dogs.

I had to fight my way through the crush to reach Tristan who was leaning across the counter in earnest conversation with a comely young barmaid. The other serving ladies were middle-aged but his practiced eye had picked this one out; glossy red hair, a puckish face and an inviting smile. I had been hoping for a soothing chat with him but he was unable to give me his undivided attention, so after juggling with a glass among the throng for a few minutes I left.

Out on the field the sun still blazed, the scent of the trampled grass rose into the warm air, the band was playing a selection from Rose Marie and peace began to steal into my soul. Maybe I could begin to enjoy the show now the pinpricks were over; there was only the Family Pets to judge and I was looking forward to that.

For about an hour I wandered among the pens of mountainous pigs and haughty sheep; the rows of Shorthorn cows with their classical wedge-shaped grace, their level udders and dainty feet.

I watched in fascination a contest which was new to me; shirt-sleeved young men sticking a fork into a straw bale and hurling it high over a bar with a jerk of their thick brown arms.

Old Steve Bramley, a local farmer, was judging the heavy horses and I envied him his massive authority as he stumped, bowler-hatted and glowering around each animal, leaning occasionally on his stick as he took stock of the points. I couldn't imagine anyone daring to argue with him.

It was late in the afternoon when the

189

loudspeaker called me to my final duty. The Family Pets contestants were arranged on wooden chairs drawn up in a wide circle on the turf. They were mainly children but behind them an interested ring of parents and friends watched me warily as I arrived.

The fashion of exotic pets was still in its infancy but I experienced a mild shock of surprise when I saw the variety of creatures on show. I suppose I must have had a vague mental picture of a few dogs and cats but I walked round the circle in growing bewilderment looking down at rabbits — innumerable rabbits of all sizes and colours — guinea pigs, white mice, several budgerigars, two tortoises, a canary, a kitten, a parrot, a Mynah bird, a box of puppies, a few dogs and cats and a goldfish in a bowl. The smaller pets rested on their owners' knees, the others squatted on the ground.

How, I asked myself, was I going to come to a decision here? How did you choose between a parrot and a puppy, a budgie and a bulldog, a mouse and a Mynah? Then as I circled it came to me;

it couldn't be done. The only way was to question the children in charge and find which ones looked after their pets best, which of them knew most about their feeding and general husbandry. I rubbed my hands together and repressed a chuckle of satisfaction; I had something to work on now.

I don't like to boast but I think I can say in all honesty that I carried out an exhaustive scientific survey of that varied group. From the outset I adopted an attitude of cold detachment, mercilessly banishing any ideas of personal preference. If I had been pleasing only myself I would have given first prize to a gleaming black Labrador sitting by a chair with massive composure and offering me a gracious paw every time I came near. And my second would have been a benevolent tabby — I have always had a thing about tabby cats — which rubbed its cheek against my hand as I talked to its owner. The pups, crawling over each other and grunting obesely, would probably have come third. But I put away these unworthy thoughts and pursued my chosen course.

I was distracted to some extent by the parrot which kept saying 'Hellow' in a voice of devastating refinement like a butler answering a telephone and the Mynah which repeatedly adjured me to 'Shut door as you go out,' in a booming Yorkshire baritone.

The only adult in the ring was a bosomy lady with glacial pop eyes and a white poodle on her knee. As I approached she gave me a challenging stare as though defying me to place her pet anywhere but first.

'Hello, little chap,' I said, extending my hand. The poodle responded by drawing its lips soundlessly back from its teeth and giving me much the same kind of look as its owner. I withdrew my hand hastily.

'Oh you needn't be afraid of him,' the lady said frigidly. 'He won't hurt you.'

I gave a light laugh. 'I'm sure he won't.' I held out my hand again. 'You're a nice little dog, aren't you?' Once more the poodle bared his teeth and when I persevered by trying to stroke his ears he snapped noiselessly, his teeth clicking

192

together an inch from my fingers.

'He doesn't like you, I can see that. Do you darling?' The lady put her cheek against the dog's head and stared at me distastefully as though she knew just how he felt.

'Shut door as you go out,' commanded the Mynah gruffly from somewhere behind me.

I gave the lady my questionnaire and moved on.

And among the throng there was one who stood out; the little boy with the goldfish. In reply to my promptings he discoursed knowledgeably about his fish, its feeding, life history and habits. He even had a fair idea of the common diseases. The bowl, too, was beautifully clean and the water fresh; I was impressed.

When I had completed the circuit I swept the ring for the last time with a probing eye. Yes, there was no doubt about it; I had the three prize winners fixed in my mind beyond any question and in an order based on strictly scientific selection. I stepped out into the middle.

'Ladies and gentlemen,' I said, scanning the company with an affable smile.

'Hellow,' responded the parrot fruitily.

I ignored him and continued. 'These are the successful entrants. First, number six, the goldfish. Second, number fifteen, the guinea pig. And third, number ten, the white kitten.'

I half expected a little ripple of applause but there was none. In fact my announcement was greeted by a tight-lipped silence. I had noticed an immediate change in the atmosphere when I mentioned the goldfish. It was striking — a sudden cold wave which swept away the expectant smiles and replaced them with discontented muttering.

I had done something wrong, but what? I looked around helplessly as the hum of voices increased. 'What do you think of that then?' 'Not fair, is it?' 'Wouldn't have thought it of him?' 'All them lovely rabbits and he hardly looked at them.'

I couldn't make it out, but my job was done, anyway. I pushed between the chairs and escaped to the open field.

'Shut door as you go out,' the Mynah requested in deepest bass as I departed.

I sought out Tristan again. The atmosphere in the beer tent had changed, too. The drinkers were long since past their peak and the hilarious babel which had met me on my last visit had died to an exhausted murmur. There was a general air of satiation. Tristan, pint in hand, was being addressed with great solemnity by a man in a flat cap and braces. The man swayed slightly as he grasped Tristan's free hand and gazed into his eyes. Occasionally he patted him on the shoulder with the utmost affection. Obviously my colleague had been forging deep and lasting friendships in here while I was making enemies outside.

I sidled up to him and spoke into his ear. 'Ready to go soon, Triss?'

He turned slowly and looked at me. 'No, old lad,' he said, articulating carefully. 'I'm afraid I shan't be coming with you. They're having a dance here on the showfield later and Doreen has consented to accompany me.' He cast a loving glance across the counter at the redhead who crinkled her nose at him.

I was about to leave when a snatch of conversation from behind made me pause.

'A bloody goldfish!' a voice was saying disgustedly.

'Aye, it's a rum 'un, George,' a second voice replied.

There was a slurping sound of beer being downed.

'But tha know, Fred,' the first voice said. 'That vet feller had to do it. Didn't 'ave no choice. He couldn't pass over t'squire's son.'

'Reckon you're right, but it's a bugger when you get graft and corruption in t'Family Pets.'

A heavy sigh, then 'It's the way things are nowadays, Fred. Everything's hulterior.'

'You're right there, George. It's hulterior, that's what it is.'

I fought down a rising panic. The Pelhams had been Lords of the Manor of Darrowby for generations and the present squire was Major Pelham. I knew him as a friendly farmer client, but that was all. I'd never heard of his son.

I clutched at Tristan's arm. 'Who is that little boy over there?'

Tristan peered out glassily across the sward. 'The one with the goldfish bowl, you mean?'

'That's right.'

'It's young Nigel Pelham, the squire's son.'

'Oh Gawd,' I moaned. 'But I've never seen him before. Where's he been?'

'Boarding school down south, I believe. On holiday just now.'

I stared at the boy again. Tousled fair hair, grey open-necked shirt, sunburned legs. Just like all the others.

George was at it again. 'Lovely dogs and cats there was, but squire's lad won it with a bloody goldfish.'

'Well let's be right,' his companion put in. 'If that lad 'ad brought along a bloody stuffed monkey he'd still 'ave got fust prize with it.'

'No doubt about it, Fred. T'other kids might as well 'ave stopped at 'ome.'

'Aye, it's not like it used to be, George.

Nobody does owt for nowt these days.'

'True, Fred, very true.' There was a gloomy silence punctuated by noisy gulpings. Then, in weary tones: 'Well you and me can't alter it. It's the kind of world we're living in today.'

I reeled out into the fresh air and the sunshine. Looking round at the tranquil scene, the long stretch of grass, the loop of pebbly river with the green hills rising behind, I had a sense of unreality. Was there any part of this peaceful cameo of rural England without its sinister undertones? As if by instinct I made my way into the long marquee which housed the produce section. Surely among those quiet rows of vegetables I would find repose.

The place was almost empty but as I made my way down the long lines of tables I came upon the solitary figure of old John William Enderby who had a little grocer's shop in the town.

'Well how are things?' I enquired.

'Nobbut middlin' lad,' the old man replied morosely.

'Why, what's wrong?'

'Well, ah got a second with me broad beans but only a highly commended for me shallots. Look at 'em.'

I looked. 'Yes, they're beautiful shallots, Mr Enderby.'

'Aye, they are, and nobbut a highly commended. It's a insult, that's what it is a insult.'

'But Mr Enderby . . . highly commended . . . I mean, that's pretty good isn't it?'

'No it isn't, it's a insult!'

'Oh bad luck.'

John William stared at me wide-eyed for a moment. 'It's not bad luck, lad, it's nowt but a twist.'

'Oh surely not!'

'Ah'm tellin' you. Jim Houlston got first with 'is shallots and judge is his wife's cousin.'

'Never!'

'It's true,' grunted John William, nodding solemnly. 'It's nowt but a twist.'

'Well I've never heard such a thing!'

'You don't know what goes on, young man. Ah wasn't even placed with me taties. Frank Thompson got first wi' that lot.' He pointed to a tray of noble tubers.

I studied them. 'I must admit they look splendid potatoes.'

'Aye, they are, but Frank pinched 'em.'

'What?'

'Aye, they took first prize at Brisby show last Thursday and Frank pinched 'em off t'stand.'

I clutched at the nearby table. The foundation of my world was crumbling. 'That can't be true, Mr Enderby.'

'Ah'm not jokin' nor jestin',' declared John William. 'Them's self and same taties, ah'd know them anywhere. It's nowt but a . . .'

I could take no more. I fled.

Outside the evening sunshine was still warm and the whole field was awash with the soft light which, in the Dales, seems to stream down in a golden flood from the high tops. But it was as if the forces of darkness were pressing on me; all I wanted was to get home.

I hurried to the stewards' tent and collected my measuring stick, running a gauntlet of hostile stares from the pony people I had outed earlier in the day. They were still waving their certificates and arguing.

On the way to the car I had to pass several of the ladies who had watched me judge the pets and though they didn't exactly draw their skirts aside they managed to convey their message. Among the rows of vehicles I spotted the man with the moustache. He still hadn't taken his terrier away and his eyes, full of wounded resentment, followed my every step.

I was opening my door when Helen and her party, also apparently on the way home, passed about fifty yards away. Helen waved, I waved back, and Richard Edmundson gave me a nod before helping her into the front seat of a gleaming, silver Daimler. The two fathers got into the back.

As I settled into the seat of my little Austin, braced my feet against the broken floor boards and squinted through the cracked windscreen I prayed that just this once the thing would go on the starter. Holding my breath I pulled at the knob but the engine gave a couple of lazy turns then fell silent.

Fishing the starting handle from under the seat I crept out and inserted it in its hold under the radiator; and as I began the old familiar winding the silver monster purred contemptuously past me and away.

Dropping into the driver's seat again I caught sight of my face in the mirror and could see the streaks and flecks of blood still caked on my cheek and around the roots of my hair. Tristan hadn't done a very good job with his bucket of cold water.

I gazed back at the emptying field and at the Daimler disappearing round a distant bend. It seemed to me that in more ways than one the show was over.

# Chapter 12

As I looked at the group of sick young cattle on the hillside a mixture of apprehension and disbelief flooded through me. Surely not more trouble for the Dalbys.

The old saw 'It never rains but it pours' seems to apply with particular force to farming. The husk outbreak last year and now this. It had all started with the death of Billy Dalby; big slow-smiling, slow-talking Billy. He was as strong and tough as any of the shaggy beasts which ranged his fields but he had just melted away in a few weeks. Cancer of the pancreas they said it was and Billy was gone before anybody could realise it and there was only his picture smiling down from the kitchen mantelpiece on his wife and three young children.

The general opinion was that Mrs Dalby should sell up and get out. You needed a man to run this place and anyway Prospect House was a bad farm. Neighbouring farmers would stick out their lower lips and shake their heads when they looked at the boggy pastures on the low side of the house with the tufts of spiky grass sticking from the sour soil or at the rocky outcrops and scattered stones on the hillside fields. No, it was a poor place and a woman would never make a go of it.

Everybody thought the same thing except Mrs Dalby herself. There wasn't much of her, in fact she must have been one of the smallest women I have ever seen — around five feet high — but there was a core of steel in her. She had her own mind and her own way of doing things.

I remember when Billy was still alive I had been injecting some sheep up there and Mrs Dalby called me into the house.

'You'll have a cup of tea, Mr Herriot?' She said it in a gracious way, not casually, her head slightly on one side and a dignified little smile on her face.

And when I went into the kitchen I knew what I would find; the inevitable tray. It was always a tray with Mrs Dalby. The hospitable Dales people were continually asking me in for some kind of refreshment — a 'bit o' dinner' perhaps, but if it wasn't midday there was usually a mug of tea and a scone or a hunk of thick-crusted apple pie — but Mrs Dalby invariably set out a special tray. And there it was today with a clean cloth and the best china cup and saucer and side plates with sliced buttered scones and iced cakes and malt bread and biscuits. It was on its own table away from the big kitchen table.

'Do sit down, Mr Herriot,' she said in her precise manner. 'I hope that tea isn't too strong for you.'

Her speech was what the farmers would call 'very proper' but it went with her personality which to me embodied a determination to do everything as correctly as possible.

'Looks perfect to me, Mrs Dalby.' I sat down feeling somewhat exposed in the middle of the kitchen with Billy smiling comfortably from an old armchair by the fire and his wife standing by my side.

She never sat down with us but stood there, very erect, hands clasped in front of her, head inclined, ceremoniously attending to my every wish. 'Let me fill your cup, Mr Herriot,' or 'Won't you try some of this custard tart?'

She wasn't what you would call pretty; it was a rough-skinned red little face with tiny, very dark eyes but there was a sweet expression and a quiet dignity. And as I say, there was strength.

Billy died in the spring and as everybody waited for Mrs Dalby to make arrangement for the sale she went right on with the running of the farm. She did it with the help of a big farm worker called Charlie who had helped Billy occasionally but now came full time. During the summer I was called out a few times for trivial ailments among the cattle and I could see that Mrs Dalby was managing to hang on; she looked a bit haggard because she was now helping in the fields and buildings as well as coping with her housework and young family, but she was still fighting.

It was half way through September

when she asked me to call to see some young cattle — stirks of around nine months — which were coughing.

'They were really fit when they were turned out in May,' she said as we walked across the grass to the gate in the corner. 'But they've really gone down badly this last week or two.'

I held the gate open, we walked through, and as I approached the group of animals I grew progressively uneasy. Even at this distance I could see that something was far wrong; they were not moving around or grazing as they should have been but were curiously immobile. There would be about thirty of them and many had their necks extended forward as if seeking air. And from the bunch a barking cough was carried to us on the soft breeze of late summer.

By the time we reached the cattle my uneasiness had been replaced by a dry-mouthed dread. They didn't seem to care as I moved in among them and I had to shout and wave my arms to get them moving; and they had barely begun to stir before the coughing broke out throughout the group; not just an occasional bark but a hacking chorus which seemed almost to be tearing the little animals apart. And they weren't just coughing; most of them were panting, standing straddle-legged, ribs heaving in a desperate fight for breath. A few showed bubbles of saliva at their lips and from here and there among the pack groans of agony sounded as the lungs laboured.

I turned as in a dream to Mrs Dalby.

'They've got husk.' Even as I said it it sounded a grimly inadequate description of the tragedy I was witnessing. Because this was neglected husk, a terrible doom-laden thing.

'Husk?' the little woman said brightly. 'What causes it?'

I looked at her for a moment then tried to make my voice casual.

'Well it's a parasite. A tiny worm which infests the bronchial tubes and sets up bronchitis — in fact that's the proper name, parasitic bronchitis. The larvae climb up the blades of grass and the cattle eat them as they graze. Some pastures are badly affected with it.' I broke off. A lecture was out of place at a time like this.

What I felt like saying was why in God's name hadn't I been called in weeks ago. Because this wasn't only bronchitis now; it was pneumonia, pleurisy, emphysema and any other lung condition you cared to name with not merely a few of the hair-like worms irritating the tubes, but great seething masses of them crawling everywhere, balling up and blocking the vital air passages. I had opened up a lot of calves like these and I knew how it looked.

I took a deep breath. 'They're pretty bad, Mrs Dalby. A mild attack isn't so bad if you can get them off the grass right away, but this has gone a long way beyond that. You can see for yourself, can't you — they're like a lot of little skeletons. I wish I'd seen them sooner.'

She looked up at me apprehensively and I decided not to belabour the point. It would be like rubbing it in; saying what her neighbours had said all along, that her inexperience would land her in trouble sooner or later. If Billy had been here he probably would never have turned his young cattle on to this marshy field; or he would have spotted the trouble right at the start and brought them inside. Charlie would be no help in a situation like this; he was a good willing chap but lived up to the Yorkshire saying, 'Strong in t'arm and thick in t'head.' Farming is a skilful business and Billy, the planner, the stocksman, the experienced agriculturist who knew his own farm inside out, just wasn't there.

Mrs Dalby drew herself up with that familiar gesture.

'Well what can we do about it, Mr Herriot?'

An honest reply in those days would have been, 'Medicinally nothing.' But I didn't say that.

'We've got to get them all inside immediately. Every mouthful of this grass is adding to the worm burden. Is Charlie around to give us a hand?'

'Yes, he's in the next field, mending a wall.' She trotted across the turf and in a minute or two returned with the big man ambling by her side.

'Aye, ah thought it were a touch of

husk,' he said amiably, then with a hint of eagerness. 'Are ye goin' to give them the throat injection?'

'Yes . . . yes . . . but let's get them up to the buildings.' As we drove the cattle slowly up the green slope I marvelled ruefully at this further example of faith in the intratracheal injection for husk. There was really no treatment for the condition and it would be another twenty years before one appeared in the shape of diethylcarbamazine, but the accepted procedure was to inject a mixture of chloroform, turpentine and creosote into the windpipe. Modern vets may raise their eyebrows at the idea of introducing this barbaric concoction directly into the delicate lung tissue and we old ones didn't think much of it either. But the farmers loved it.

When we had finally got the stirks into the fold yard I looked round them with something like despair. The short journey had exacerbated their symptoms tremendously and I stood in the middle of a symphony of coughs, grunts and groans while the cattle, tongues protruding, ribs pumping, gasped for breath.

I got a bottle of the wonderful injection from the car, and with Charlie holding the head and little Mrs Dalby hanging on to the tail I began to go through the motions. Seizing the trachea in my left hand I inserted the needle between the cartilaginous rings and squirted a few c.c.'s into the lumen and, as always, the stirk gave a reflex cough, sending up the distinctive aroma of the medicaments into our faces.

'By gaw, you can smell it straight off, guvnor,' Charlie said with deep satisfaction. 'Ye can tell it's gettin' right to t'spot.'

Most of the farmers said something like that. And they had faith, the books spoke comfortably about the chloroform stupefying the worms, the turpentine killing them and the creosote causing increased coughing which expelled them. But I didn't believe a word of it. The good results which followed were in my opinion due entirely to bringing the animals in from the infected pasture.

But I knew I had to do it and we injected

every animal in the yard. There were thirty two of them and Mrs Dalby's tiny figure was involved in the catching of all of them; clutching vainly at their necks, grabbing their tails, pushing them up against the wall. William, the eldest son, aged eight, came in from school and he plunged into the fray by his mother's side.

My repeated 'Be careful, Mrs Dalby!' or Charlie's gruff 'Watch thissen, Missis, or you'll get lamed!' had no effect. During the melee both she and the little boy were kicked, trodden on and knocked down but they never showed the slightest sign of being discouraged.

At the end, the little woman turned to me, her face flushed to an even deeper hue. Panting, she looked up, 'Is there anything else we can do, Mr Herriot?'

'Yes there is.' In fact the two things I was going to tell her were the only things which ever did any good. 'First, I'm going to leave you some medicine for the worms which are in the stomach. We can get at them there, so Charlie must give every stirk a dose. Secondly, you'll have to start giving them the best possible food — good hay and high protein cake.'

Her eyes widened. 'Cake? That's expensive stuff. And hay . . .'

I knew what she was thinking. The precious hay safely garnered for next winter's feed; to have to start using it now was a cruel blow, especially with all that beautiful grass out there; grass, the most natural, most perfect food for cattle but every blade carrying its own load of death.

'Can't they go out again . . . ever?' she asked in a small voice.

'No, I'm sorry. If they had just had a mild attack you could have kept them in at nights and turned them out after the dew had left the grass in the mornings. The larvae climb up the grass mainly when it's wet. But your cattle have got too far. We daren't risk them picking up any more worms.'

'Right . . . thank you, Mr Herriot. We know where we are, anyway.' She paused. 'Do you think we'll lose any of them?'

My stomach contracted into a tight ball. I had already told her to buy cake she couldn't afford and it was a certainty she would have to lay out more precious cash for hay in the winter. How was I going to tell her that nothing in the world was going to stop this batch of beasts dying like flies? When animals with husk started blowing bubbles it was nearly hopeless and the ones which were groaning with every breath were quite simply doomed. Nearly half of them were in these two categories and what about the rest? The pathetic barking other half? Well, they had a chance.

'Mrs Dalby,' I said. 'It would be wrong of me to make light of this. Some of them are going to die, in fact unless there's a miracle you are going to lose quite a few of them.' At the sight of her stricken face I made an attempt to be encouraging. 'However, where there's life there's hope and sometimes you get pleasant surprises at this job.' I held up a finger. 'Worm them and get some good grub into them! That's your hope — to help them to fight it off themselves.'

'I see.' She lifted her chin in her characteristic way. 'And now you must come in for a wash.'

And of course there it was in its usual place in the kitchen; the tray with all the trimmings.

'Really, Mrs Dalby. You shouldn't have bothered. You have enough to do without this.'

'Nonsense,' she said, the smile back on her face. 'You take one spoonful of sugar don't you?'

As I sat there she stood in her habitual position, hands clasped in front of her, watching me while the middle boy, Dennis, who was five looked up at me solemnly and Michael, a mere toddler of two, fell over the coal scuttle and started to bawl lustily.

The usual procedure was to repeat the intratracheal injection in four days so I had to go through with it. Anyway, it gave me a chance to see how the cattle were faring.

When I drew up in the yard my first sight was of a long sack-covered mound on the cobbles. A row of hooves protruded from beneath the sacks. I had expected something of the sort but the reality was still like a blow in the face. It was still quite early in the morning and perhaps I wasn't feeling quite strong enough to have the evidence of my failure thrust before my eyes. Because failure it undoubtedly was; even though I had been in a hopeless position from the start there was something damning in those motionless hooves jutting from their rough blanket.

I made a quick count. There were four dead cattle under there. Wearily I made my way into the fold yard; I had no cheerful expectation of what I would find inside. Two of the stirks were down and unable to rise from the deep straw, the rest were still panting, but I noticed with a faint lifting of my gloom that several of them were doggedly munching at the cubes of cake in the troughs and others were pulling an occasional wisp of hay from the racks. It was incredible how animals with advanced respiratory symptoms would still eat; and it provided the only gleam of hope.

I walked over to the house. Mrs Dalby greeted me cheerfully as though those carcases outside didn't exist.

'It's time for the second injection,' I

said, and then after some hesitation, 'I see you've lost four of them . . . I'm sorry.'

'Well you told me, Mr Herriot.' She smiled through the tired lines on her face. 'You said I had to expect it so it wasn't as big a shock as it might have been.' She finished washing the youngest child's face, seized a towel in her work-roughened hands and rubbed him briskly, then she straightened up. It was Saturday and William was at home and I noticed not for the first time that there was something about the little boy which suggested that even at his age he had decided he was going to be the man about the house. He pulled on his little wellingtons and marched resolutely with us across the yard to do his bit as he saw it. I rested my hand on his shoulder as he walked beside me; he would have to grow up a lot more rapidly than most youngsters but I had the feeling that the realities of life wouldn't bowl him over very easily.

We gave the animals their second injection with the two little Dalbys again throwing themselves fearlessly into the rough and tumble and that was about the last practical thing I did in the husk outbreak.

Looking back, there is a macabre fascination in recalling situations like this when we veterinary surgeons were utterly helpless in the face of inevitable disaster. Nowadays, thank heavens, the young members of the profession do not have to stand among a group of gasping, groaning creatures with the sick knowledge that they can't do a thing about it; they have an excellent oral vaccine to prevent husk and efficient therapeutic agents to treat it.

But with the Dalbys who needed my help so desperately I had nothing to offer; my memories are of repeated comfortless visits, of death, and of an all-pervading reek of chloroform, creosote and turpentine. When the business had finally come to an end a dozen of the stirks had died, about five were alive but blowing hard and would probably be stunted and unthrifty for the rest of their lives. The rest, thanks to the good feeding and not to my treatment, had recovered.

It was a crushing blow for any farmer to take but for a widow struggling to survive it could have been fatal. But on my last visit little Mrs Dalby, hovering as usual, hands clasped, above the tea tray, was undefeated.

'Only them as has them can lose them,' she said firmly, her head tilted as always.

I had heard that said many times and they were brave Yorkshire words. But I wondered . . . did she have enough to be able to lose so many?

She went on. 'I know you've told me not to turn the young beasts on to that field next year but isn't there anything we can give them to stop them getting husk?'

'No, Mrs Dalby, I'm sorry.' I put down my cup. 'I don't think there's anything country vets need and want more than a husk vaccine. People keep asking us that question and we have to keep on saying no.'

We had to keep on saying no for another twenty years as we watched disasters like I had just seen at the Dalbys', and the strange thing is that now we have a first rate vaccine it is taken completely for granted.

Driving away I stopped to open the gate at the end of the track and looked back at the old stone farmhouse crouching against the lower slopes. It was a perfect autumn day with mellow golden sunshine softening the harsh sweep of fell and moor with their striding walls and the air so still and windless that the whirring of a pigeon's wings overhead was loud in the silence. Across the valley on the hilltop a frieze of sparse trees stood as motionless as though they had been painted across the blue canvas of sky.

It seemed wrong that in the midst of this beauty was worry and anxiety, grinding struggle and the threat of ruin. I closed the gate and got back into the car. That little woman over there may have weathered this calamity but as I started the engine the thought was strong in my mind that another such thing would finish her.

# Chapter 13

I was vastly relieved when winter came and spring followed and I saw virtually nothing of Mrs Dalby. It was one market day in midsummer that she came to the surgery. I was just going to open the door when Siegfried beat me to it. More than most people he appreciated the hospitality we were shown on the farms and he had sampled Mrs Dalby's tray as often as I had. On top of that he had the deepest admiration for her indomitable battle to keep the farm going for her children, so that whenever she appeared at Skeldale House he received her like royalty. His manners, always impeccable, became those of a Spanish grandee.

I watched him now as he threw the door wide and hurried to the top step.

'Why, Mrs Dalby! How very nice to see you! Do come inside.' He extended his hand towards the house.

The little woman, dignified as ever, inclined her head, smiled and walked past him while Siegfried hastened to her side; and as they negotiated the passage he kept up a running fire of enquiries. 'And how is William . . . and Dennis . . . and little Michael? Good, good, splendid.'

At the sitting room door there was the same ceremonious opening and courteous gestures and once inside a tremendous scraping of armchairs as he hauled them around to make sure she was comfortable and in the right position.

Next he galloped through to the kitchen to organise some refreshment and when Mrs Hall appeared with the tray he raked it with an anxious glance as though he feared it may fall below the standard of Mrs Dalby's. Apparently reassured, he poured the tea, hovered around solicitously for a moment or two then sat down opposite, the very picture of rapt attention.

The little woman thanked him and sipped at her cup.

'Mr Farnon, I have called to see you

about some young beasts. I turned a batch of thirty five out this spring and they looked in good condition but now they're losing ground fast — all of them.'

My heart gave a great thump and something must have shown in my face because she smiled across at me.

'Oh don't worry, Mr Herriot, it's not husk again. There's not a cough among the lot of them. But they are going thin and they're badly scoured.'

'I think I know what that will be,' Siegfried said, leaning across to push a plate of Mrs Hall's flapjack towards her. 'They'll have picked up a few worms. Not lungworms but the stomach and intestinal kind. They probably just need a good dose of medicine to clear them out.'

She nodded and took a piece of the flapjack. 'Yes, that's what Charlie thought and we've dosed the lot of them. But it doesn't seem to have made any difference.'

'That's funny.' Siegfried rubbed his chin. 'Mind you they sometimes need a repeat but you should have seen some improvement. Perhaps we'd better have a look at them.'

'That's what I would like,' she said. 'It would set my mind at rest.'

Siegfried opened the appointment book. 'Right, and the sooner the better. Tomorrow morning all right? Splendid.' He made a quick note then looked up at her. 'By the way I'm going off for a week's holiday starting this evening, so Mr Herriot will be coming.'

'That will be fine,' she replied, turning to me and smiling without a trace of doubt or misgiving. If she was thinking 'This is the fellow who supervised the deaths of nearly half of my young stock last year' she certainly didn't show it. In fact when she finally finished her tea and left she waved and smiled again as though she could hardly wait to see me again.

And when I walked across the fields with Mrs Dalby next day it was like turning the clock back to last year, except that we were going in the other direction; not down towards the marshy ground below the house but up to the stony pastures which climbed in an uneven checkerboard between their stone walls

225

over the lower slopes of the hill.

The similarity persisted as we approached, too. These young beasts — roans, reds, red and whites — were an almost exact counterpart of last year's batch; shaggy little creatures, little more than calves, they stood spindly legged and knock-kneed regarding us apathetically as we came up the rise. And though their symptoms were entirely different from the previous lot there was one thing I could say for sure; they were very ill.

As I watched I could see the dark watery diarrhoea flowing from them without any lifting of the tails as though there was nothing they could do to control it. And every one of them was painfully thin, the skin stretched over the jutting pelvic bones and the protruding rows of ribs.

'I haven't neglected them this time,' Mrs Dalby said. 'I know they look dreadful but this seems to have happened within a few days.'

'Yes . . . yes . . . I see . . .' My eyes were hunting desperately among the little animals trying to find some sort of clue. I had seen unthriftiness from parasitism but nothing like this.

'Have you kept a lot of cattle in these fields over the last year or two?' I asked.

She paused in thought for a moment. 'No . . . no . . . I don't think so. Billy used to let the milk cows graze up here now and then but that's all.'

The grass wouldn't be likely to be 'sick' with worms, then. In any case it didn't look like that. What it did look like was Johne's disease, but how in God's name could thirty five young things like this get Johne's at the same time? Salmonella . . . ? Coccidiosis. . . ? Some form of poisoning, perhaps . . . this was the time of year when cattle ate strange plants. I walked slowly round the field, but there was nothing unusual to be seen; it took even the grass all its time to grow on these wind-blown hillsides and there was no great range of other herbage. I could see bracken higher up the fell but none down here; Billy would have cleared it years ago.

'Mrs Dalby,' I said. 'I think you'd better give these stirks another dose of the worm medicine just to be sure and in the meantime I'm going to take some samples of the manure for examination at the laboratory.'

I brought up some sterile jars from the car and went painstakingly round the pasture scooping up as wide a range as possible from the pools of faeces.

I took them to the lab myself and asked them to phone the results through. The call came within twenty four hours; negative for everything. I resisted the impulse to dash out to the farm immediately; there was nothing I could think of doing and it wouldn't look so good for me to stand there gawping at the beasts and scratching my head. Better to wait till tomorrow to see if the second dose of worm medicine did any good. There was no reason why it should, because none of the samples showed a pathogenic worm burden.

In these cases I always hope that inspiration will come to me as I am driving around or even when I am examining other animals but this time as I climbed from the car outside Prospect

House I was barren of ideas.

The young beasts were slightly worse. I had decided that if I still couldn't think of anything I would give the worst ones vitamin injections more or less for the sake of doing something; so with Charlie holding the heads I inserted the hypodermic under the taut skins of ten of the little creatures, trying at the same time to put away the feeling of utter futility. We didn't have to drive them inside; they were easily caught in the open field and that was a bad sign in itself.

'Well you'll let me know, Mrs Dalby,' I said hoarsely as I got back into the car. 'If that injection improves them I'll do the lot.' I gave what I hoped was a confident wave and drove off.

I felt so bad that it had a numbing effect on me and over the next few days my mind seemed to shy away from the subject of the Dalby stirks as though by not thinking about them they would just go away. I was reminded that they were still very much there by a phone call from Mrs Dalby.

'I'm afraid my cattle aren't doing any good, Mr Herriot.' Her voice was strained.

I grimaced into the receiver. 'And the ones I injected. . . ?'

'Just the same as the others.'

I had to face up to reality now and drove out to Prospect House immediately; but the feeling of cold emptiness, of having nothing to offer, made the journey a misery. I hadn't the courage to go to the farm house and face Mrs Dalby but hurried straight up through the fields to where the young beasts were gathered.

And when I walked among them and studied them at close range the apprehension I had felt on the journey was nothing to the sick horror which rushed through me now. Another catastrophe was imminent here. The big follow-up blow which was all that was needed to knock the Dalby family out once and for all was on its way. These animals were going to die. Not just half of them like last year but all of them, because there was hardly any variation in their symptoms; there didn't seem to be a single one of them which was fighting off the disease.

But what disease? God almighty, I was a veterinary surgeon! Maybe not steeped in experience but I wasn't a new beginner any more. I should surely have some small inkling why a whole great batch of young beasts was sinking towards the knacker yard in front of my eyes.

I could see Mrs Dalby coming up the field with little William striding in his tough, arm-swinging way by her side and Charlie following behind.

What the hell was I going to say to them? Shrug my shoulders with a light laugh and say I hadn't a single clue in my head and that it would probably be best to phone Mallock now and ask them to shoot the lot of them straight away for dog meat? They wouldn't have any cattle to bring on for next year but that wouldn't matter because they would no longer be farming.

Stumbling among the stricken creatures I gazed at them in turn, almost choking as I looked at the drooping, sunken-eyed heads, the gaunt little bodies, the eternal trickle of that deadly scour. There was a curious immobility about the group, probably because they were too weak to walk about; in fact as I watched, one of them took a few steps, swayed and almost fell.

Charlie was pushing open the gate into the field just a hundred yards away. I turned and stared at the nearest animal, almost beseeching it to tell me what was wrong with it, where it felt the pain, how this thing had all started. But I got no response. The stirk, one of the smallest, only calf-size, with a very dark roan-coloured head showed not the slightest interest but gazed back at me incuriously through its spectacles. What was that . . . what was I thinking about . . . spectacles? Was my reason toppling. . . ? But yes, by God, he did have spectacles . . . a ring of lighter hair surrounding each eye. And that other beast over there . . . he was the same. Oh glory be, now I knew! At last I knew!

Mrs Dalby, panting slightly, had reached me.

'Good morning, Mr Herriot,' she said, trying to smile. 'What do you think, then?'

She looked around the cattle with anxious eyes.

'Ah, good morning to you, Mrs Dalby,' I replied expansively, fighting down the impulse to leap in the air and laugh and shout and perhaps do a few cartwheels. 'Yes, I've had a look at them and it is pretty clear now what the trouble is.'

'Really? Then what. . . ?'

'It's copper deficiency.' I said it casually as though I had been turning such a thing over in my mind right from the beginning. 'You can tell by the loss of the pigment in the coat, especially around the eyes. In fact when you look at them you can see that a lot of them are a bit paler than normal.' I waved a airy hand in the general direction of the stirks.

Charlie nodded. 'Aye, by gaw, you're right. Ah thowt they'd gone a funny colour.'

'Can we cure it?' Mrs Dalby asked the inevitable question.

'Oh yes, I'm going straight back to the surgery now to make up a copper mixture and we'll dose the lot. And you'll have to repeat that every fortnight while they are out at grass. It's a bit of a nuisance, I'm afraid, but there's no other way. Can you do it?'

'Oh aye, we'll do it,' Charlie said.

And 'Oh aye, we'll do it,' little William echoed, sticking out his chest and strutting around aggressively as though he wanted to start catching the beasts right away.

The treatment had a spectacular effect. I didn't have the modern long-lasting copper injections at my disposal but the solution of copper sulphate which I concocted under the surgery tap at Skeldale House worked like magic. Within a few weeks that batch of stirks was capering, lively and fully fleshed, over those hillside fields. Not a single death, no lingering unthriftiness. It was as though the whole thing had never happened, as though the hand of doom had never hovered over, not only over the cattle, but the little family of humans.

It had been a close thing and, I realised, only a respite. That little woman had a long hard fight ahead of her still.

I have always abhorred change of any kind but it pleases me to come forward twenty years and spectate at another morning in the kitchen at Prospect House. I was seated at the same little table picking a buttered scone from the same tray and wondering whether I should follow it with a piece of malt bread or one of the jam tarts.

Billy still smiled down from the mantelpiece and Mrs Dalby, hands clasped in front of her, was watching me, her head a little on one side, the same half smile curving her lips. The years had not altered her much; there was some grey in her hair but the little red, weathered face and the bright eyes were as I had always known them.

I sipped my tea and looked across at the vast bulk of William sprawled in his father's old chair, smiling his father's smile at me. There were about fifteen stones of William and I had just been watching him in action as he held a fully grown bullock's hind foot while I examined it. The animal had made a few attempts to kick but the discouragement

235

on its face had been obvious as William's great hands effortlessly engulfed its fetlock and a corner of his wide shoulder span dug into its abdomen.

No, I couldn't expect William to be the same, nor Dennis and Michael clattering into the kitchen now in their heavy boots and moving over to the sink to wash their hands. They were six footers too with their father's high-shouldered easy slouching walk but without William's sheer bulk.

Their tiny mother glanced at them then up at the picture on the mantelpiece.

'It would have been our thirtieth anniversary today,' she said conversationally.

I looked at her, surprised. She never spoke of such things and I didn't know how to answer. I couldn't very well say 'congratulations' when she had spent twenty of those years alone. She had never said a word about her long fight; and it had been a winning fight. She had bought the neighbouring farm lower down the Dale when old Mr Mason retired; it was a good farm with better land and

William had lived there after his marriage and they ran the two places as one. Things were pretty good now with her three expert stocksmen sons eliminating the need for outside labour except old Charlie who still pottered around doing odd jobs.

'Yes, thirty years,' Mrs Dalby said, looking slowly round the room as though she was seeing it for the first time. Then she turned back and bent over me, her face serious.

'Mr Herriot,' she said, and I was sure that at last, on this special day, she was going to say something about the years of struggle, the nights of worry and tears, the grinding toil.

For a moment she rested her hand lightly on my shoulder and her eyes looked into mine.

'Mr Herriot, are you quite sure that tea is to your liking?'

# Chapter 14

One of the things Helen and I had to do was furnish our bed-sitter and kitchen. And when I say 'furnish' I use the word in its most austere sense. We had no high-flown ideas about luxury; it was, after all, a temporary arrangement and anyway we had no money to throw around.

My present to Helen at the time of our marriage was a modest gold watch and this had depleted my capital to the extent that a bank statement at the commencement of our married life revealed the sum of twenty five shillings standing to my credit. Admittedly I was a partner now but when you start from scratch it takes a long time to get your head above water.

But we did need the essentials like a table, chairs, cutlery, crockery, the odd rug and carpet, and Helen and I decided that it would be most sensible to pick up these things at house sales. Since I was constantly going round the district I was able to drop in at these events and the duty of acquiring our necessities had been delegated to me. But after a few weeks it was clear that I was falling down on the job.

I had never realised it before but I had a blind spot in these matters. I would go to a sale and come away with a pair of brass candlesticks and a stuffed owl. On another occasion I acquired an ornate inkwell with a carved metal figure of a dog on it together with a polished wooden box with unnumerable fascinating little drawers and compartments for keeping homeopathic prescriptions. I could go on for a long time about the things I bought but they were nearly all useless.

Helen was very nice about it.

'Jim,' she said one day when I was proudly showing her a model of a fully rigged sailing ship in a bottle which I had been lucky enough to pick up. 'It's lovely, but I don't think we need it right now.'

I must have been a big disappointment to the poor girl and also to the local auctioneers who ran the sales. These gentlemen, when they saw me hovering around the back of the crowd would cheer up visibly. They, in common with most country folk, thought all vets were rich and that I would be bidding for some of the more expensive items. When a nice baby grand piano came up they would look over the heads at me with an expectant smile and their disappointment was evident when I finally went away with a cracked-faced barometer or a glove stretcher.

A sense of my failure began to seep through to me and when I had to take a sample through to the Leeds Laboratory I saw a chance to atone.

'Helen,' I said, 'there's a huge sale room right in the city centre. I'll take an hour off and go in there. I'm bound to see something we need.'

'Oh good!' my wife replied. 'That's a great idea! There'll be lots to choose from there. You haven't had much chance to find anything at those little country sales.' Helen was always kind.

After my visit to the Leeds lab I asked

the way to the sale rooms.

'Leave your car here,' one of the locals advised me. 'You'll never park in the main street and you can get a tram right to the door.'

I was glad I listened to him because when I arrived the traffic was surging both ways in a nonstop stream. The saleroom was at the top of an extraordinarily long flight of smooth stone steps leading right to the top of the building. When I arrived, slightly out of breath, I thought immediately I had come to the right place, a vast enclosure strewn with furniture, cookers, gramophones, carpets — everything you could possibly want in a house.

I wandered around fascinated for quite a long time then my attention centred on two tall piles of books quite near to where the auctioneer was selling. I lifted one of them. It was The Geography of the World. I had never seen such beautiful books; as big as encyclopaedias and with thick embossed covers and gold lettering. The pages, too, were edged with gold and the paper was of a delightfully smooth texture. Quite enthralled I turned the pages, marvelling at the handsome illustrations, the coloured pictures each with its covering transparent sheet. They were a little old-fashioned, no doubt, and when I looked at the front I saw they were printed in 1858; but they were things of beauty.

Looking back, I feel that fate took a hand here because I had just reluctantly turned away when I heard the auctioneer's voice.

'Now then, here's a lovely set of books. The Geography of the World in Twenty Four Volumes. Just look at them. You don't find books like them today. Who'll give me a bid?'

I agreed with him. They were unique. But they must be worth pounds. I looked round the company but nobody said a word.

'Come on, ladies and gentlemen, surely somebody wants this wonderful addition to their library. Now what do I hear?'

Again the silence then a seedy looking man in a soiled mackintosh spoke up.

'Arf a crown,' he said morosely.

I looked around expecting a burst of laughter at this sally, but nobody was amused. In fact the auctioneer didn't seem surprised.

'I have a half a crown bid.' He glanced about him and raised his hammer. With a thudding of the heart I realised he was going to sell.

I heard my own voice, slightly breathless. 'Three shillings.'

'I have a bid of three shillings for The Geography of the World in Twenty Four Volumes. Are you all done?' Bang went the hammer. 'Sold to the gentleman over there.'

They were mine! I couldn't believe my luck. This surely was the bargain to end all bargains. I paid my three shillings while one of the men tied a length of rough string round each pile. The first pause in my elation came when I tried to lift my purchases. Books are heavy things and these were massive specimens; and there were twenty four of them.

With a hand under each string I heaved like a weight-lifter and, pop-eyed, veins standing out on my forehead, I managed to get them off the ground and began to stagger shakily to the exit.

The first string broke on the top step and twelve of my volumes cascaded downwards over the smooth stone. After the first moment of panic I decided that the best way was to transport the intact set down to the bottom and come back for the others. I did this but it took me some time and I begun to perspire before I was all tied up again and poised on the kerb ready to cross the road.

The second string broke right in the middle of the tram lines as I attempted a stiff-legged dash through a break in the traffic. For about a year I scrabbled there in the middle of the road while horns hooted, tram bells clanged and an interested crowd watched from the sidewalks. I had just got the escaped volumes balanced in a column and was reknotting the string when the other lot burst from their binding and slithered gently along the metal rails; and it was when I was retrieving them that I noticed a large policeman, attracted by the din and the long line of vehicles, walking with measured strides in my direction.

In my mental turmoil I saw myself for the first time in the hands of the law. I could be done on several charges — Breach of the Peace, Obstructing Traffic to name only two — but I perceived that the officer was approaching very slowly and rightly or wrongly I feel that when a policeman strolls towards you like that he is a decent chap and is giving you a chance to get away. I took my chance. He was still several yards off when I had my two piles reassembled and I thrust my hands under the strings, tottered to the far kerb and lost myself in the crowd.

When I finally decided there was no longer any fear of feeling the dread grip on my shoulder I stopped in my headlong flight and rested in a shop doorway. I was puffing like a broken-winded horse and my hands hurt abominably. The sale room string was coarse, hairy and abrasive and already it threatened to take the skin off my fingers.

Anyway, I thought, the worst was over. The tram stop was just at the end of the block there. I joined the queue and when the tram arrived, shuffled forward with the others. I had one foot on the step when a large hand was thrust before my eyes.

Just a minute, brother, just a minute! Where d'you think you're goin'?' The face under the conductor's hat was the meaty, heavy jowled, pop-eyed kind which seems to take a mournful pleasure in imparting bad news.

'You're not bringin' that bloody lot on 'ere, brother, I'll tell tha now!'

I looked up at him in dismay. 'But . . . It's just a few books . . .'

'Few books! You want a bloody delivery van for that lot. You're not usin' my tram — passengers couldn't stir inside!' His mouth turned down aggressively.

'Oh but really,' I said with a ghastly attempt at an ingratiating smile, 'I'm just going as far as . . .'

'You're not goin' anywhere in 'ere, brother! Ah've no time to argue — move your foot, ah'm off!'

The bell ding-dinged and the tram began to move. As I hopped off backwards one of the strings broke again.

After I had got myself sorted out I

surveyed my situation and it appeared fairly desperate. My car must be over a mile away, mostly uphill, and I would defy the most stalwart Nepalese Sherpa to transport these books that far. I could of course just abandon the things; lean them against this wall and take to my heels . . . But no, that would be anti-social and anyway they were beautiful. If only I could get them home all would be well.

Another tram rumbled up to the stop and again I hefted my burden and joined the in-going passengers, hoping nobody would notice.

It was a female voice this time.

'Sorry, you can't come on, luv.' She was middle-aged, motherly and her plump figure bulged her uniform tightly.

'We don't 'ave delivery men on our trams. It's against t'rules.'

I repressed a scream. 'But I'm not a . . . these are my own books. I've just bought them.'

'Bought 'em?' Her eyebrows went up as she stared at the dusty columns.

'Yes . . . and I've got to get them home somehow.'

'Well somebody'll tek 'em home for you luv. Hasta got far to go?'

'Darrowby.'

'Eee, by gun, that's a long way. Right out in t'country.' She peered into the tram's interior. 'But there isn't no room in there, luv.'

The passengers had all filed in and I was left alone standing between my twin edifices; and the conductress must have seen a desperate light in my eyes because she made a sudden gesture.

'Come on then, luv! You can stand out 'ere on the platform wi' me. I'm not supposed to, but ah can't see you stuck there.'

I didn't know whether to kiss her or burst into tears. In the end I did neither but stacked the books in a corner of the platform and stood swaying over them till we arrived at the park where I had left my car.

The relief at my deliverance was such that I laughed off the few extra contretemps on my way to the car. There were in fact several more spills before I had the books tucked away on the back seat but when I finally drove away I felt like singing.

It was when I was threading my way through the traffic that I began to rejoice that I lived in the country, because the car was filled with an acrid reek which I thought could only come from the conglomeration of petrol fumes and industrial smoke. But even when the city had been left behind and I was climbing into the swelling green of the Pennines the aroma was still with me.

I wound down the window and gulped greedily as the sweet grassy air flowed in but when I closed it the strange pungency returned immediately. I stopped, leaned over and sniffed at the region of the back seat. And there was no doubt about it; it was the books.

Ah well, they must have been kept in a damp place or something like that. I was sure it would soon pass off. But in the meantime it certainly was powerful; it nearly made my eyes water.

I had never really noticed the long climb to our eyrie on top of Skeldale House but it was different today. I suppose my arms and shoulders were finally beginning to feel the strain and that string, bristly but fragile, was digging into my hands harder than ever, but it was true that every step was an effort and when I at last gained the top landing I almost collapsed against the door of our bed-sitter.

When, perspiring and dishevelled, I entered, Helen was on her knees, dusting the hearth. She looked up at me expectantly.

'Any luck, Jim?'

'Yes, I think so,' I replied with a trace of smugness. 'I think I got a bargain.'

Helen rose and looked at me eagerly. 'Really?'

'Yes' I decided to play my trump card. 'I only had to spend three shillings!'

'Three shillings! What . . . where. . . ?'

'Wait there a minute.' I went out to the landing and put my hand under those strings. This, thank heaven, would be the last time I would have to do this. A lunge and a heave and I had my prizes through the doorway and displayed for my wife's inspection.

She stared at the two piles. 'What have you got there?'

'The Geography of the World in Twenty Four Volumes,' I replied triumphantly.

'The Geography of the . . . and is that all?'

'Yes, couldn't manage anything else, I'm afraid. But look — aren't they magnificent books!'

My wife's level gaze had something of disbelief, a little of wonder. For a moment one corner of her mouth turned up then she coughed and became suddenly brisk.

'Ah well, we'll have to see about getting some shelves for them. Anyway, leave them there for now.' She went over and kneeled again by the hearth. But after a minute or two she paused in her dusting.

'Can you smell anything funny?'

'Well, er . . . I think it's the books, Helen. They're just a bit musty . . . I don't think it'll last long.'

But the peculiar exhalation was very pervasive and it was redolent of extreme age. Very soon the atmosphere in our room was that of a freshly opened mausoleum.

I could see Helen didn't want to hurt my feelings but she kept darting looks of growing alarm at my purchases. I decided to say it for her.

'Maybe I'd better take them downstairs just for now.'

She nodded gratefully.

The descent was torture, made worse by the fact that I had thought I was finished with such things. I finally staggered into the office and parked the books behind the desk. I was panting and rubbing my hands when Siegfried came in.

'Ah, James, had a nice run through to Leeds?'

'Yes, they said at the lab that they'd give us a ring about those sheep as soon as they've cultured the organisms.'

'Splendid!' My colleague opened the door of the cupboard and put some forms inside then he paused and began to sniff the air.

'James, there's a bloody awful stink in here.'

I cleared my throat. 'Well yes, Siegfried, I bought a few books while I was in Leeds. They seem a little damp.' I pointed behind the desk.

Siegfried's eyes widened as he looked at the twin edifices. 'What the devil are they?'

I hesitated. 'The Geography of the World in Twenty Four Volumes.'

He didn't say anything but looked from me to the books and back again. And he kept sniffing. There was no doubt that only his innate good manners were preventing him from telling me to get the damn things out of here.

'I'll find a place for them,' I said, and with a great weariness pushed my hands yet again under the strings. My mind was in a ferment as I shuffled along the passage. What in heaven's name was I going to do with them? But as I passed the cellar door on my right it seemed to provide the answer.

There were great vaulted chambers beneath Skeldale House, a proper wine cellar in the grand days. The man who went down there to read the gas meter always described them as 'The Cattycombs' and as I descended into the murky, dank-smelling depths I thought sadly that it was a fitting resting place for my books. We kept only coal and wood down here now and from the muffled thuds I judged that Tristan was chopping logs.

He was a great log chopper and when I rounded the corner he was whirling his axe expertly round his head. He stopped when he saw me with my burden and asked the inevitable question.

I answered for, I hoped, the last time. 'The Geography of the World in Twenty Four Volumes.' And I followed with a blow by blow account of my story.

As he listened he opened one tome after another, sniffed at it and replaced it hurriedly. And he didn't have to tell me, I knew already. My cherished books were down here to stay.

But the compassion which has always been and still is uppermost among the many facets of Tristan's character came to the fore now.

'Tell you what, Jim,' he said 'We can put them in there.' He pointed to a dusty wine bin just visible in the dimlight which filtered through the iron grating at the top of the coal chute which led from the street.

'It's just like a proper book shelf.'

He began to lift the volumes into the bin and when he had arranged them in a long row he ran his finger along the faded opulence of the bindings.

'There now, they look a treat in there, Jim.' He paused and rubbed his chin. 'Now all you want is somewhere to sit. Let's see now . . . ah, yes!' He retreated into the gloom and reappeared with an armful of the biggest logs. He made a few more journeys and in no time had rigged up a seat for me within arm's reach of the books.

'That'll do fine,' he said with deep satisfaction.

'You can come down here and have a read whenever you feel like it.'

And that is how it turned out. The books never came up those steps again but quite frequently when I had a few minutes to spare and wanted to improve my mind I went down and sat on Tristan's seat in the twilight under the grating and renewed my acquaintance with The Geography of the World in Twenty Four Volumes.

# Chapter 15

The flu epidemic sweeping through the Darrowby district hit the farming folk particularly hard. The townspeople could take a few days off till it passed but when there were cows to be milked twice a day it couldn't be done. On my rounds I saw stocksmen flushed with fever, staggering streaming-eyed from cow to cow when they should have been in bed.

Helen's father and Auntie Lucy were two of the victims and in need of help. I didn't wait for Helen to say anything about it but suggested right away that she should return to the farm for a few days to run the house. And it was so strange in the bed-sitter without her that I went back downstairs to my old room adjoining Tristan's to sleep and I ate with the brothers in the big dining room.

I was sitting at breakfast one morning with the feeling of having turned back the clock. My partner was refilling my coffee cup when his brother cleared his throat.

'You know, there's maybe something in this Raynes Ghost business after all.' Tristan pushed his chair back from the breakfast table, stretched out his legs more comfortably and resumed his study of the *Darrowby and Houlton Times*. 'It says here they've got a historian looking into it and this man has unearthed some interesting facts.'

Siegfried didn't say anything, but his eyes narrowed as his brother took out a Woodbine and lit it. Siegfried had given up smoking a week ago and he didn't want to watch anybody lighting up; particularly somebody like Tristan who invested even the smallest action with quiet delight, rich fulfilment. My partner's mouth tightened to a grim line as the young man unhurriedly selected a cigarette, flicked his lighter and dragged the smoke deep with a kind of ecstatic gasp.

'Yes,' Tristan continued, thin outgoing wisps mingling with his words. 'This chap points out that several of the monks were murdered at Raynes Abbey in the fourteenth century.'

'Well, so what?' snapped Siegfried.

Tristan raised his eyebrows. 'This cowled figure that's been seen so often lately near the abbey — why shouldn't it be the spirit of one of those monks?'

'Whaat? What's that you say?'

'Well, after all it makes you think, doesn't it? Who knows what fell deeds might have been. . . ?'

'What the hell are you talking about?' Siegfried barked.

Tristan looked hurt. 'That's all very well, and you may laugh, but remember what Shakespeare said.' He raised a solemn finger. 'There are more things in heaven and earth, Horatio, than are dreamt of in your . . .'

'Oh balls!' said Siegfried, bringing the discussion effectively to a close.

I took a last thankful swallow of coffee and put down my cup. I was pleased that the topic had petered out fairly peacefully because Siegfried was in an edgy condition. Up to last week he had been a dedicated puffer of pipe and cigarettes but he had also developed a classical smoker's cough and had suffered increasingly from violent stomach-ache. At times his long thin face had assumed the appearance of a skull, the cheeks deeply sunken, the eyes smouldering far down in their sockets. And the doctor had said he must give up smoking.

Siegfried had obeyed, felt immediately better and was instantly seized with the evangelical zeal of the convert. But he didn't just advise people to give up tobacco; I have seen him several times strike a cigarette from the trembling fingers of farm workers, push his face to within inches of theirs and grind out menacingly, 'Now don't ever let me see you with one of those bloody things in your mouth again, do you hear?'

Even now there are grizzled men who tell me with a shudder, 'Nay, ah've never had a fag sin' Mr Farnon told me to stop, thirty years back. Nay, bugger it, the way 'e looked at me I dursn't do it!'

However the uncomfortable fact remained that his crusade hadn't the slightest effect on his brother. Tristan smoked almost continually but he never coughed and his digestion was excellent.

Siegfried looked at him now as he contentedly tapped off a little ash and took another blissful suck. 'You smoke too many of those bloody cigarettes!'

'So do you.'

'No I don't!' Siegfried retorted. 'I'm a non-smoker and it's time you were, too! It's a filthy habit and you'll kill yourself the way you're going!'

Tristan gave him a benign look and again his words floated out on the fine Woodbine mist. 'Oh I'm sure you're wrong. Do you know, I think it rather agrees with me.'

Siegfried got up and left the room. I sympathised with him for he was in a difficult position. Being in loco parentis he was in a sense providing his brother with the noxious weeds and his innate sense of propriety prevented him from abusing his position by dashing the things from Tristan's hands as he did with others. He had to fall back on exhortation and it was getting him nowhere. And there was another thing — he probably wanted to avoid a row this morning as Tristan was leaving on one of his mysterious trips back to the Veterinary College; in fact my first job was to take him down to the Great North Road where he was going to hitch a lift.

After I had left him there I set off on my rounds and, as I drove, my thoughts kept going back to the conversation at breakfast. A fair number of people were prepared to swear that they had seen the Raynes ghost and though it was easy to dismiss some of them as sensation mongers or drunkards the fact remained that others were very solid citizens indeed.

The story was always the same. There was a hill beyond Raynes village and at the top a wood came right up to the roadside. Beyond lay the abbey. People driving up the hill late at night said they had seen the monk in their headlights — a monk in a brown habit just disappearing into the wood. They believed the figure had been walking across the road but they weren't sure because it was always a little too far away. But they were

262

adamant about the other part; they had seen a cowled figure, head bowed, go into that wood. There must have been something uninviting about the apparition because nobody ever said they had gone into the wood after it.

It was strange that after my thoughts had been on Raynes during the day I should be called to the village at one o'clock the following morning. Crawling from bed and climbing wearily into my clothes I couldn't help thinking of Tristan curled up peacefully in his Edinburgh lodgings far away from the troubles of practice. But I didn't feel too bad about getting up; Raynes was only three miles away and the job held no prospect of hard labour — a colic in a little boy's Shetland pony. And it was a fine night — very cold with the first chill of autumn but with a glorious full moon to light my way along the road.

They were walking the pony round the yard when I got there. The owner was the accountant at my bank and he gave me a rueful smile.

'I'm very sorry to get you out of bed, Mr

Herriot, but I was hoping this bit of bellyache would go off. We've been parading round here for two hours. When we stop he tries to roll.'

'You've done the right thing,' I said. 'Rolling can cause a twist in the bowel.' I examined the little animal and was reassured. He had a normal temperature, good strong pulse, and listening at his flank I could hear the typical abdominal sounds of spasmodic colic.

What he needed was a good evacuation of the bowel, but I had to think carefully when computing the dose of arecoline for this minute member of the equine species. I finally settled on an eighth of a grain and injected it into the neck muscles. The pony stood for a few moments in the typical colic position, knuckling over and sinking down on one hind leg then the other and occasionally trying to lie down.

'Walk him on again slowly will you?' I was watching for the next stage and I didn't have long to wait; the pony's jaws began to champ and his lips to slobber and soon long dribbles of saliva hung down from his mouth. All right so far but I had to wait another fifteen minutes before he finally cocked his tail and deposited a heap of faeces on the concrete of the yard.

'I think he'll be O.K. now,' I said. 'So I'll leave you to it. Give me another ring if he's still in pain.'

Beyond the village the road curved suddenly out of sight of the houses then began the long straight climb to the abbey. Just up there at the limits of my headlights would be where the ghost was always seen — walking across the road and into the black belt of trees. At the top of the hill, on an impulse, I drew in to the side of the road and got out of the car. This was the very place. At the edge of the wood, under the brilliant moon, the smooth boles of the beeches shone with an eerie radiance and, high above, the branches creaked as they swayed in the wind.

I walked into the wood, feeling my way carefully with an arm held before me till I came out on the other side. Raynes Abbey lay before me.

I had always associated the beautiful ruin with summer days with the sun warming the old stones of the graceful arches, the chatter of voices, children playing on the cropped turf; but this was 2.30 a.m. in an empty world and the cold breath of the coming winter on my face. I felt suddenly alone.

In the cold glare everything was uncannily distinct. But there was a look of unreality about the silent rows of columns reaching into the dark sky and throwing their long pale shadows over the grass. Away at the far end I could see the monks' cells — gloomy black caverns deep in shadow — and as I looked an owl hooted, accentuating the heavy, blanketing silence.

A prickling apprehension began to creep over me, a feeling that my living person had no place here among these brooding relics of dead centuries. I turned quickly and began to hurry through the wood, bumping into the trees, tripping over roots and bushes, and when I reached my car I was trembling and more out of breath than I should have been. It was good to slam the door, turn the ignition and hear the familiar roar of the engine.

I was home within ten minutes and trotted up the stairs, looking forward to catching up on my lost sleep. Opening my bedroom door I flicked on the switch and felt a momentary surprise when the room remained in darkness. Then I stood frozen in the doorway.

By the window, where the moonlight flooded in, making a pool of silver in the gloom, a monk was standing. A monk in a brown habit, motionless, arms folded, head bowed. His face was turned from the light towards me but I could see nothing under the drooping cowl but a horrid abyss of darkness.

I thought I would choke. My mouth opened but no sound came. And in my racing mind one thought pounded above the others — there were such things as ghosts after all.

Again my mouth opened and a hoarse shriek emerged.

'Who in the name of God is that?'

The reply came back immediately in a sepulchral bass.

'Tristaan.'

I don't think I actually swooned, but I

did collapse limply across my bed and lay there gasping, the blood thundering in my ears. I was dimly aware of the monk standing on a chair and screwing in the light bulb, giggling helplessly the while. Then he flicked on the switch and sat on my bed. With his cowl pushed back on his shoulders he lit a Woodbine and looked down at me, still shaking with laughter.

'Oh God, Jim, that was marvellous — even better than I expected.'

I stared up at him and managed a whisper. 'But you're in Edinburgh . . .'

'Not me, old lad. There wasn't much doing so I concluded my business and hitched straight back, I'd just got in when I saw you coming up the garden. Barely had time to get the bulb out and climb into my outfit — I couldn't miss the opportunity.'

'Feel my heart,' I murmured.

Tristan rested his hand on my ribs for a moment and as he felt the fierce hammering a fleeting concern crossed his face.

'Hell, I'm sorry, Jim.' Then he patted my shoulder reassuringly. 'But don't worry. If it was going to be fatal you'd have dropped down dead on the spot. And anyway, a good fright is very beneficial — acts like a tonic. You won't need a holiday this year.'

'Thanks,' I said. 'Thanks very much.'

'I wish you could have heard yourself.' He began to laugh again. 'That scream of terror . . . oh dear, oh dear!'

I hoisted myself slowly into a sitting position, pulled out the pillow, propped it against the bed head and leaned back against it. I still felt very weak.

I eyed him coldly. 'So you're the Raynes ghost.'

Tristan grinned in reply but didn't speak.

'You young devil! I should have known. But tell me, why do you do it? What do you get out of it?'

'Oh I don't know.' The young man gazed dreamily at the ceiling through the cigarette smoke. 'I suppose it's just getting the timing right so that the drivers aren't quite sure whether they've seen me or not. And then I get a hell of a kick out of hearing them revving up like mad and roaring off for home. None of them ever slows down.'

'Well, somebody once told me your sense of humour was overdeveloped,' I said. 'And I'm telling you it'll land you in the cart one of these days.'

'Not a chance. I keep my bike behind a hedge about a hundred yards down the road so that I can make a quick getaway if necessary. There's no problem.'

'Well, please yourself.' I got off the bed and made shakily for the door. 'I'm going downstairs for a tot of whisky, and just remember this.' I turned and glared at him. 'If you try that trick on me again I'll strangle you.'

A few days later at about eight o'clock in the evening I was sitting reading by the fireside in the big room at Skeldale House when the door burst open and Siegfried burst into ther room.

'James,' he rapped out. 'Old Horace Dawson's cow has split its teat. Sounds like a stiching job. The old chap won't be able to hold the cow and he has no near neighbors to help him so I wonder if you'd

270

come and give me a hand.'

'Sure, glad to.' I marked the place in my book, stretched and yawned then got up from the chair. I noticed Siegfried's foot tapping on the carpet and it occurred to me, not for the first time, that the only thing that would satisfy him would be some kind of ejector seat on my chair which would hurl me straight through the door and into action at the word of command. I was being as quick as I could but I had the feeling as always — when I was writing something for him or operating under his eyes — that I wasn't going nearly fast enough. There were elements of tension in the knowledge that the mere fact of watching me rise from the chair and replace my book in the fireside alcove was an almost unbearable strain for him.

By the time I was half way across the carpet he had disappeared into the passage. I followed at a trot and just made it into the street as he was starting the car. Grabbing the door I made a dive for the interior and felt the road whip away from under my foot as we took off into the darkness.

Fifteen minutes later we screeched to a halt in the yard behind a little smallholding standing on its own across a couple of fields. The engine had barely stopped before my colleague was out of the car and striding briskly towards the cow house. He called to me over his shoulder as he went.

'Bring the suture materials, James, will you . . . and the local and syringe . . . and that bottle of wound lotion . . .'

I heard the brief murmur of conversation from within then Siegfried's voice again, raised this time in an impatient shout.

'James! What are you doing out there? Can't you find those things?'

I had hardly got the boot open and I rummaged frantically among the rows of tins and bottles. I found what he required, galloped across the yard and almost collided with him as he came out of the building.

He was in mid shout. 'James! What the hell's keeping you . . . oh, you're there. Right, let's have that stuff . . . what have you been doing all this time?'

He had been right about Horace Dawson, a tiny frail man of about eighty who couldn't be expected to do any strong-arm stuff. Despite his age he had stubbornly refused to give up milking the two fat shorthorn cows which stood in the little cobbled byre.

Our patient had badly damaged a teat; either she or her neighbour must have stood on it because there was a long tear running almost full length with the milk running from it.

'It's a bad one, Horace,' Siegfried said. 'You can see it goes right into the milk channel. But we'll do what we can for her — t'll need a good few stiches in there.'

He bathed and disinfected the teat then filled a syringe with local anaesthetic.

'Grab her nose, James,' he said, then spoke gently to the farmer. 'Horace, will you please hold her tail for me. Just catch it by the very end, that the way . . . lovely.'

The little man squared his shoulders. 'Aye, ah can do that fine, Mr Farnon.'

'Good lad, Horace, that's splendid,

thank you. Now stand well clear.' He bent over and as I gripped the animal's nose he inserted the needle above the top extremity of the wound.

There was an instant smacking sound as the cow registered her disapproval by kicking Siegfried briskly half way up his wellington boot. He made no sound but breathed deeply and flexed his knee a couple of times before crouching down again.

'Cush pet,' he murmured soothingly as he stuck the needle in again.

This time the cloven foot landed on his forearm, sending the syringe winging gracefully through the air till it came to rest by a piece of good fortune in the hay-rack. Siegfried straightened up, rubbed his arm thoughtfully, retrieved his syringe and approached the patient again.

For a few moments he scratched around the root of her tail and addressed her in the friendliest manner. 'All right, old lady, it isn't very nice, is it?'

When he got down again he adopted a new stance, burrowing with his head into the cow's flank and stretching his long arms high he managed despite a few more near misses to infiltrate the tissues round the wound with local. Then he proceeded to thread a needle unhurriedly, whistling tunelessly under his breath.

Mr Dawson watched him admiringly. 'Ah know why you're such a good feller wi' animals, Mr Farnon. It's because you're so patient — I reckon you're t'patientest man ah've ever seen.'

Siegfried inclined his head modestly and recommenced work. And it was more peaceful now. The cow couldn't feel a thing as my colleague put in a long, even row of stiches, pulling the lips of the wound firmly together.

When he had finished he put an arm round the old man's shoulders.

'Now, Horace, if that heals well the teat will be as good as new. But it won't heal if you pull at it, so I want you to use this tube to milk her.' He held up a bottle of spirit in which a teat syphon gleamed.

'Very good,' said Mr Dawson firmly. 'Ah'll use it.'

Siegfried wagged a playful finger in his face. 'But you've got to be careful, you know. You must boil the tube every time before use and keep it always in the bottle or you'll finish up with mastitis. Will you do that?'

'Mr Farnon,' the little man said, holding himself very erect. 'Ah'll do exackly as you say.'

'That's my boy, Horace.' Siegfried gave him a final pat on the back before starting to pick up his instruments. 'I'll pop back in about two weeks to take the stiches out.'

As we were leaving, the vast form of Claude Blenkiron loomed suddenly in the byre door. He was the village policeman, though obviously off duty judging by the smart check jacket and slacks.

'I saw you had summat on, Horace, and I wondered if you wanted a hand.'

'Nay, thank ye, Mr Blenkiron. It's good of ye but you're ower late. We've done t'job,' the old man replied.

Siegfried laughed. 'Wish you'd arrived half an hour ago, Claude. You could have tucked this cow under your arm while I stitched her.'

The big man nodded and a slow smile

spread over his face. He looked the soul of geniality but I felt, as always, that there was a lot of iron behind that smile. Claude was a well-loved character in the district, a magnificent athlete who bestowed lavish help and friendship on all who needed it on his beat. But though he was a sturdy prop to the weak and the elderly he was also a merciless scourge of the ungodly.

I had no first hand knowledge but there were rumours that Claude preferred not to trouble the magistrates with trivialities but dispensed his own form of instant justice. It was said that he kept a stout stick handy and acts of hooliganism and vandalism were rapidly followed by a shrill yowling down some dark alley. Second offenders were almost unknown and in fact his whole district was remarkably law-abiding. I looked again at the smiling face. He really was the most pleasant looking man but as I say there was something else there and nothing would ever have induced me to pick a fight with him.

'Right, then,' he said. 'I was just on me

way into Darrowby so I'll say good night gentlemen.'

Siegfried put a hand on his arm. 'Just a moment, Claude, I want to go on to see another of my cases. I wonder if you'd give Mr Herriot a lift into the town.'

'I'll do that with pleasure, Mr Farnon,' the policeman replied and beckoned me to follow him.

In the darkness outside I got into the passenger seat of a little Morris Eight and waited for a few moments while Claude squeezed his bulk behind the wheel. As we set off he began to talk about his recent visit to Bradford where he had been taking part in a wrestling match.

We had to go through Raynes village on the way back and as we left the houses behind the ascent to the abbey he suddenly stopped talking. Then he startled me as he snapped upright in his seat and pointed ahead.

'Look, look there, it's that bloody monk!'

'Where? Where?' I feigned ignorance but I had seen it all right — the cowled, slow-pacing figure heading for the wood.

Claude's foot was on the boards and the car was screaming up the hill. At the top he swung savagely on to the roadside grass so that the headlights blazed into the depth of the wood and as he leapt from the car there was a fleeting moment when his quarry was in full view; a monk, skirts hitched high, legging it with desperate speed among the trees.

The big man reached into the back of the car and pulled out what looked like a heavy walking stick. 'After the bugger!' he shouted, plunging eagerly forward.

I panted after him. 'Wait a minute, what are you going to do if you catch him?'

'I'm goin' to come across his arse with me ash plant,' Claude said with chilling conviction and galloped ahead of me till he disappeared from the circle of light. He was making a tremendous noise, beating against the tree trunks and emitting a series of intimidating shouts.

My heart bled for the hapless spectre blundering in the darkness with the policeman's cries dinning in his ears. I waited with tingling horror for the final confrontation and the tension increased as time passed and I could still hear Claude in full cry; 'Come out of there, you can't get away! Come on, show yourself!' while his splintering blows echoed among the trees.

I did my own bit of searching but found nothing. The monk did indeed seem to have disappeared and when I finally returned to the car I found the big man already there.

'Well that's a rum 'un, Mr Herriot,' he said. 'I can't find 'im and I can't think where he's got to. I was hard on his heels when I first spotted him and he didn't get out of the wood because I can see over the fields in the moonlight. I've 'ad a scout round the abbey too, but he isn't there. He's just bloody vanished.'

I was going to say something like 'Well, what else would you expect from a ghost?' but the huge hand was still swinging that stick and I decided against it.

'Well I reckon we'd better get on to Darrowby,' the policeman grunted, stamping his feet on the frosty turf. I shivered. It was bitterly cold with an east wind getting up and I was glad to climb back into the car.

In Darrowby I had a few companionable beers with Claude at his favorite haunt, the Black Bull, and it was ten thirty when I got into Skeldale House. There was no sign of Tristan and I felt a twinge of anxiety.

It must have been after midnight when I was awakened by a faint scuffling from the next room. Tristan occupied what had been the long, narrow 'dressing room' in the grand days when the house was young. I jumped out of bed and opened the communicating door.

Tristan was in pyjamas and he cuddled two hot water bottles to his bosom. He turned his head and gave me a single haggard glance before pushing one of the bottles well down the bed. Then he crawled between the sheets and lay on his back with the second bottle clasped across his chest and his eyes fixed on the ceiling. I went over and looked down at him in some concern. He was shaking so much that the whole bed vibrated with him.

'How are you, Triss?' I whispered.

After a few moments a faint croak came up. 'Frozen to the bloody marrow, Jim.'

'But where the heck have you been?'

Again the croak. 'In a drainpipe.'

'A drainpipe!' I stared at him. 'Where?'

The head rolled feebly from side to side on the pillow. 'Up at the wood. Didn't you see those pipes by the roadside?'

A great light flashed. 'Of course, yes! They're going to put a new sewer into the village, aren't they?'

'That's right,' Tristan whispered. 'When I saw that big bloke pounding into the wood I cut straight back and dived into one of the pipes. God only knows how long I was in there.'

'But why didn't you come out after we left?'

A violent shudder shook the young man's frame and he closed his eyes briefly. 'I couldn't hear a thing in there. I was jammed tight with my cowl over my ears and there was a ninety mile an hour wind screaming down the pipe. I didn't hear the car start and I daren't come out in case that chap was still standing there with his bloody great shillelagh.' He took hold of the quilt with one hand and picked at it fitfully.

'Well never mind, Triss,' I said. 'You'll soon get warmed up and you'll be all right after a night's sleep.'

Tristan didn't appear to have heard. 'They're horrible things, drainpipes, Jim.' He looked up at me with hunted eyes. 'They're full of muck and they stink of cats' pee.'

'I know, I know.' I put his hand back inside the quilt and pulled the sheets up round his chin. 'You'll be fine in the morning.' I switched off the light and tiptoed from the room. As I closed the door I could still hear his teeth chattering.

Clearly it wasn't only the cold that was bothering him; he was still in a state of shock. And no wonder. The poor fellow had been enjoying a little session of peaceful haunting with never a care in the world when without warning there was a scream of brakes a blaze of light and that giant bounding into the middle of it like the demon king. It had all been too much.

Next morning at the breakfast table

Tristan was in poor shape. He looked very pale, he ate little and at intervals his body was racked by deep coughing spasms.

Siegfried looked at him quizzically. 'I know what's done this to you. I know why you're sitting there like a zombie, coughing your lungs up.'

His brother stiffened in his chair and a tremor crossed his face. 'You do?'

'Yes, I hate to say I told you so, but I did warn you, didn't I? It's all those bloody cigarettes!'

Tristan never did give up smoking but the Raynes ghost was seen no more and remains an unsolved mystery to this day.

# Chapter 16

This was one for Granville Bennett. I liked a bit of small animal surgery and was gradually doing more as time went on but this one frightened me. A twelve year old spaniel bitch in the last stages of pyometritis, pus dripping from her vulva on to the surgery table, temperature a hundred and four, panting, trembling, and, as I held my stethoscope against her chest I could hear the classical signs of valvular insufficiency. A dicky heart was just what I needed on top of everything else.

'Drinking a lot of water, is she?' I asked.

Old Mrs Barker twisted the strings of her shopping bag anxiously. 'Aye, she never seems to be away from the water bowl. But she won't eat — hasn't had a bite for the last four days.'

'Well I don't know,' I took off my

stethoscope and stuffed it in my pocket. 'You should have brought her in long ago. She must have been ill for weeks.'

'Not rightly ill, but a bit off it. I thought there was nothing to worry about as long as she was eating.'

I didn't say anything for a few moments. I had no desire to upset the old girl but she had to be told.

'I'm afraid this is rather serious, Mrs Barker. The condition has been building up for a long time. It's in her womb, you see, a bad infection, and the only cure is an operation.'

'Well will you do it, please?' The old lady's lips quivered.

I came round the table and put my hand on her shoulder.

'I'd like to, but there are snags. She's in poor shape and twelve years old. Really a poor operation risk. I'd like to take her through to the Veterinary Hospital at Hartington and let Mr Bennett operate on her.

'All right,' she said, nodding eagerly. 'I don't care what it costs.'

'Oh we'll keep it down as much as

possible.' I walked along the passage with her and showed her out of the door. 'Leave her with me — I'll look after her, don't worry. What's her name, by the way?'

'Dinah,' she replied huskily, still peering past me down the passage.

I went through and lifted the phone. Thirty years ago country practitioners had to turn to the small animal experts when anything unusual cropped in that line. It is different nowadays when our practices are more mixed. In Darrowby now we have the staff and equipment to tackle any type of small animal surgery but it was different then. I had heard it said that sooner or later every large animal man had to scream for help from Granville Bennett and now it was my turn.

'Hello, is that Mr Bennett?'

'It is indeed.' A big voice, friendly, full of give.

'Herriot here. I'm with Farnon in Darrowby.'

'Of course! Heard of you, laddie, heard of you.'

'Oh . . . er . . . thanks. Look, I've got a

bit of a sticky job here. I wonder if you'd take it on for me.'

'Delighted, laddie, what is it?'

'A real stinking pyo.'

'Oh lovely!'

'The bitch is twelve years old.'

'Splendid!'

'And toxic as hell.'

'Excellent!'

'And one of the worst hearts I've heard for a long time.'

'Fine, fine! When are you coming through?'

'This evening, if it's O.K. with you. About eight.'

'Couldn't be better, laddie. See you.'

Hartington was a fair sized town — about 200,000 inhabitants — but as I drove into the centre the traffic had thinned and only a few cars rolled past the rows of shop fronts. I hoped my twenty five mile journey had been worth it. Dinah, stretched out on a blanket in the back, looked as if she didn't care either way. I glanced behind me at the head drooping over the edge of the seat, at the white muzzle and the cataracts in her eyes gleaming palely in the light from the dash. She looked so old. Maybe I was wasting my time, placing too much faith in this man's reputation.

There was no doubt Granville Bennett had become something of a legend in northern England. In those days when specialisation was almost unknown he had gone all out for small animal work — never looked at farm stock — and had set a new standard by the modern procedures in his animal hospital which was run as nearly as possible on human lines. It was, in fact, fashionable for veterinary surgeons of that era to belittle dog and cat work; a lot of the older men who had spent their lives among the teeming thousands of draught horses in city and agriculture would sneer 'Oh I've no time to bother with those damn things.' Bennett had gone dead in the opposite direction.

I had never met him but I knew he was a young man in his early thirties. I had heard a lot about his skill, his business acumen, and about his reputation as a bon viveur. He was, they said, a dedicated devotee of the work-hard-play-hard school.

The Veterinary Hospital was a long low building near the top of a busy street. I drove into a yard and knocked at a door in the corner. I was looking with some awe at a gleaming Bentley dwarfing my own battered little Austin when the door was opened by a pretty receptionist.

'Good evening,' she murmured with a dazzling smile which I thought must be worth another half crown on the bill for a start. 'Do come in, Mr Bennett is expecting you.'

I was shown into a waiting room with magazines and flowers on a corner table and many impressive photographs of dogs and cats on the walls — taken, I learned later, by the principal himself. I was looking closely at a superb study of two white poodles when I heard a footstep behind me. I turned and had my first view of Granville Bennett.

He seemed to fill the room. Not over tall but of tremendous bulk. Fat, I thought at first, but as he came nearer it seemed to me that the tissue of which he was composed wasn't distributed like fat. He wasn't flabby, he didn't stick out in any particular place, he was just a big wide, solid, hard-looking man. From the middle of a pleasant blunt-featured face the most magnificent pipe I had ever seen stuck forth shining and glorious, giving out delicious wisps of expensive smoke. It was an enormous pipe, in fact it would have looked downright silly with a smaller man but on him it was a thing of beauty. I had a final impression of a beautifully cut dark suit and sparkling shirt cuffs as he held out a hand.

'James Herriot!' He said it as somebody else might have said 'Winston Churchill.'

'That's right.'

'Well, this is grand. Jim, is it?'

'Well yes, usually.'

'Lovely. We've got everything laid on for you, Jim. The girls are waiting in the theatre.'

'That's very kind of you, Mr Bennett.'

'Granville, Granville please!' He put his arm through mine and led me to the operating room.

Dinah was already there, looking very

woebegone. She had had a sedative injection and her head nodded wearily. Bennett went over to her and gave her a swift examination.

'Mm, yes, let's get on, then.'

The two girls went into action like cogs in a smooth machine. Bennett kept a large lay staff and these animal nurses, both attractive, clearly knew what they were about. While one of them pulled up the anaesthetic and instrument trolleys the other seized Dinah's foreleg expertly above the elbow, raised the radial vein by pressure and quickly clipped and disinfected the area.

The big man strolled up with a loaded needle and effortlessly slipped the needle into the vein.

'Pentothal,' he said as Dinah slowly collapsed and lay unconscious on the table. It was one of the new short-acting anaesthetics which I had never seen used.

While Bennett scrubbed up and donned sterilised gown and cap the girls rolled Dinah on her back and secured her there with ties to loops on the operating table. They applied the ether and oxygen mask to her face then shaved and swabbed the operation site. The big man returned in time to have a scalpel placed in his hand.

With almost casual speed he incised skin and muscle layers and when he went through the peritoneum the horns of the uterus which in normal health would have been two slim pink ribbons now welled into the wound like twin balloons, swollen and turgid with pus. No wonder Dinah had felt ill, carrying that lot around with her.

The stubby fingers tenderly worked round the mass, ligated the ovarian vessels and uterine body then removed the whole thing and dropped it into an enamel bowl. It wasn't till he had begun to stitch that I realised that the operation was nearly over though he had been at the table for only a few minutes. It would all have looked childishly easy except that his total involvement showed in occasional explosive commands to the nurses.

And as I watched him working under the shadowless lamp with the white tiled walls around him and the rows of instruments gleaming by his side it came to me with a rush of mixed emotions that this was what I had always wanted to do myself. My dreams when I had first decided on veterinary work had been precisely of this. Yet here I was, a somewhat shaggy cow doctor; or perhaps more correctly a farm physician, but certainly something very different. The scene before me was a far cry from my routine of kicks and buffets, of muck and sweat. And yet I had no regrets; the life which had been forced on me by circumstances had turned out to be a thing of magical fulfilment. It came to me with a flooding certainty that I would rather spend my days driving over the unfenced roads of the high country than stooping over that operating table.

And anyway I couldn't have been a Bennett. I don't think I could have matched his technique and this whole set up was eloquent of a lot of things like business sense, foresight and driving ambition which I just didn't possess.

My colleague was finished now and was fitting up an intravenous saline drip. He taped the needle down in the vein then turned to me.

'That's it, then, Jim. It's up to the old girl now.' He began to lead me from the room and it struck me how very pleasant it must be to finish your job and walk away from it like this. In Darrowby I'd have been starting now to wash the instruments, scrub the table, and the final scene would have been of Herriot the great surgeon swilling the floor with mop and bucket. This was a better way.

Back in the waiting room Bennett pulled on his jacket and extracted from a side pocket the immense pipe which he inspected with a touch of anxiety as if he feared mice had been nibbling at it in his absence. He wasn't satisfied with his examination because he brought forth a soft yellow cloth and began to polish the briar with intense absorption. Then he held the pipe high, moving it slightly from side to side, his eyes softening at the play of the light on the exquisite grain. Finally he produced a pouch of mammoth proportions, filled the bowl, applied a match with a touch of reverence and closed his eyes as a fragrant mist drifted from his lips.

'That baccy smells marvellous,' I said. 'What is it?'

'Navy Cut DeLuxe.' He closed his eyes again. 'You know, I could eat the smoke.'

I laughed. 'I use the ordinary Navy Cut myself.'

He gazed at me like a sorrowing Buddha. 'Oh you mustn't, laddie, you mustn't. This is the only stuff. Rich . . . fruity . . .' His hand made languid motions in the air. 'Here, you can take some away with you.'

He pulled open a drawer. I had a brief view of a stock which wouldn't have disgraced a fair sized tobacconist's shop; unnumerable tins, pipes, cleaners, reamers, cloths.

'Try this,' he said. 'And tell me if I'm not right.'

I looked down at the first container in my hand. 'Oh but I can't take all this. It's a four ounce tin!'

'Rubbish, my boy. Put it in your pocket.' He became suddenly brisk. 'Now I expect you'll want to hang around till old Dinah comes out of the anaesthetic so why don't we have a quick beer? I'm a member of a nice little club just across the road.'

'Well fine, sounds great.'

He moved lightly and swiftly for a big man and I had to hurry to keep up with him as he left the surgery and crossed to a building on the other side of the street.

# Chapter 17

Inside the club was masculine comfort, hails of welcome from some prosperous looking members and a friendly greeting from the man behind the bar.

'Two pints, Fred,' murmured Bennett absently, and the drinks appeared with amazing speed. My colleague poured his down apparently without swallowing and turned to me.

'Another, Jim?'

I had just tried a sip at mine and began to gulp anxiously at the bitter ale. 'Right, but let me get this one.'

'No can do, laddie.' He glanced at me with mild severity. 'Only members can buy drinks. Same again, Fred.'

I found I had two glasses at my elbow and with a tremendous effort I got the first one down. Gasping slightly I was surveying the second one timidly when I noticed that Bennett was three quarters down his. As I watched he drained it effortlessly.

'You're slow, Jim,' he said, smiling indulgently. 'Just set them up again will you, Fred.'

In some alarm I watched the barman ply his handle and attacked my second pint resolutely. I surprised myself by forcing it over my tonsils then, breathing heavily, I got hold of the third one just as Bennett spoke again.

'We'll just have one for the road, Jim,' he said pleasantly. 'Would you be so kind, Fred?'

This was ridiculous but I didn't want to appear a piker at our first meeting. With something akin to desperation I raised the third drink and began to suck feebly at it. When my glass was empty I almost collapsed against the counter. My stomach was agonisingly distended and a light perspiration had broken out on my brow. As I almost lay there I saw my colleague moving across the carpet towards the door.

'Time we were off, Jim,' he said. 'Drink up.'

It's wonderful what the human frame can tolerate when put to the test. I would have taken bets that it was impossible for me to drink that fourth pint without at least half an hour's rest, preferably in the prone position, but as Bennett's shoe tapped impatiently I tipped the beer a little at a time into my mouth, feeling it wash around my back teeth before incredibly disappearing down my gullet. I believe the water torture was a favourite with the Spanish Inquisition and as the pressure inside me increased I knew just how their victims felt.

When I at last blindly replaced my glass and splashed my way from the bar the big man was holding the door open. Outside in the street he placed an arm across my shoulder.

'The old Spaniel won't be out of it yet,' he said. 'We'll just slip to my house and have a bite — I'm a little peckish.'

Sunk in the deep upholstery of the Bentley, cradling my swollen abdomen in my arms I watched the shop fronts flicker past the windows and give way to the darkness of the open countryside. We drew up outside a fine grey stone house in a typical Yorkshire village and Bennett ushered me inside.

He pushed me towards a leather armchair. 'Make yourself at home, laddie. Zoe's out at the moment but I'll get some grub.' He bustled through to the kitchen and reappeared in seconds with a deep bowl which he placed on a table by my side.

'You know, Jim,' he said, rubbing his hands. 'There's nothing better after beer than a few pickled onions.'

I cast a timorous glance into the bowl. Everything in this man's life seemed to be larger than life, even the onions. They were bigger than golf balls, brownish-white, glistening.

'Well thanks Mr Ben . . . Granville.' I took one of them, held it between finger and thumb and stared at it helplessly. The beer hadn't even begun to sort itself out inside me; the idea of starting on this potent-looking vegetable was unthinkable.

Granville reached into the bowl, popped an onion into his mouth, crunched it quickly, swallowed and sank his teeth into a second. 'By God, that's good. You know, my little wife's a marvellous cook. She even makes pickled onions better than anyone.

Munching happily he moved over to the sideboard and clinked around for a few moments before placing in my hand a heavy cut glass tumbler about two thirds full of neat whisky. I couldn't say anything because I had taken the plunge and put the onion in my mouth; and as I bit boldly into it the fumes rolled in a volative wave into my nasal passages, making me splutter. I took a gulp at the whisky and looked up at Granville with watering eyes.

He was holding out the onion bowl again and when I declined he regarded it for a moment with hurt in his eyes. 'It's funny you don't like them, I always thought Zoe did them marvellously.'

'Oh you're wrong, Granville, they're delicious. I just haven't finished this one.'

He didn't reply but continued to look at the bowl with gentle sorrow. I realized there was nothing else for it; I took another onion.

Immensely gratified, Granville hurried through to the kitchen again. This time when he came back he bore a tray with an enormous cold roast, a loaf of bread, butter and mustard.

'I think a beef sandwich would go down rather nicely, Jim,' he murmured as he stropped his carving knife on a steel. Then he noticed my glass of whisky still half full.

'C'mon, c'mon, c'mon!' he said with some asperity, 'You're not touching your drink.' He watched me benevolently as I drained the glass then he refilled it to its old level. 'That's better. And have another onion.'

I stretched my legs out and rested my head on the back of the chair in an attempt to ease my internal turmoil. My stomach was a lake of volcanic lava bubbling and popping fiercely in its crater with each additional piece of onion, every sip of whisky setting up a fresh violent reaction. Watching Granville at work, a great wave of nausea swept over me. He was sawing busily at the roast, carving off slices which looked to be an inch thick, slapping mustard on them and enclosing them in the bread. He hummed with contentment as the pile grew. Every now and then he had another onion.

'Now then, laddie,' he cried at length, putting a heaped plate at my elbow. 'Get yourself round that lot.' He took his own supply and collapsed with a sigh into another chair.

He took a gargantuan bite and spoke as he chewed. 'You know, Jim, this is something I enjoy — a nice little snack. Zoe always leaves me plenty to go at when she pops out.' He engulfed a further few inches of sandwich. 'And I'll tell you something, though I say it myself, these are bloody good, don't you think so?'

'Yes indeed.' Squaring my shoulders I bit, swallowed and held my breath as another unwanted foreign body slid down to the ferment below.

Just then I heard the front door open.

'Ah, that'll be Zoe,' Granville said and was about to rise when a disgracefully fat Staffordshire Bull Terrier burst into the room, waddled across the carpet and leaped into his lap.

'Phoebles, my dear, come to daddykins!' he shouted. 'Have you had nice walkies with mummy?'

The Staffordshire was closely followed by a Yorkshire Terrier which was also enthusiastically greeted by Granville.

'Yoo-hoo, Victoria, Yoo-hoo!'

The Yorkie, an obvious smiler, did not jump up but contented herself with sitting at her master's feet, baring her teeth ingratiatingly every few seconds.

I smiled through my pain. Another myth exploded; the one about these specialist small animal vets not being fond of dogs themselves. The big man crooned over the two little animals. The fact that he called Phoebe 'Phoebles' was symptomatic.

I heard light footsteps in the hall and looked up expectantly. I had Granville's wife typed neatly in my mind; domesticated, devoted, homely; many of these dynamic types had wives like that, willing slaves content to lurk in the background. I waited confidently for the entrance of a plain little hausfrau.

When the door opened I almost let my vast sandwich fall. Zoe Bennett was a glowing warm beauty who would make any man alive stop for another look. A lot of soft brown hair, large grey-green friendly eyes, a tweed suit sitting sweetly on a slim but not too slim figure; and something else, a wholesomeness, an inner light which made me wish suddenly that I was a better man or at least that I looked better than I did.

In an instant I was acutely conscious of the fact that my shoes were dirty, that my old jacket and corduroy trousers were out of place here. I hadn't troubled to change but had rushed straight out in my working clothes, and they were different from Granville's because I couldn't go round the farms in a suit like his.

'My love, my love!' he carolled joyously as his wife bent over and kissed him fondly. 'Let me introduce Jim Herriot from Darrowby.'

The beautiful eyes turned on me.

'How d'you do, Mr Herriot!' she looked as pleased to see me as her husband had done and again I had the desperate wish that I was more presentable; that my hair was combed, that I didn't have this mounting conviction that I was going to explode into a thousand pieces at any moment.

'I'm going to have a cup of tea, Mr Herriot. Would you like one?'

'No-no, no, no, thank you very much but no, no, not at the moment.' I backed away slightly.

'Ah well, I see you've got one of Granville's little sandwiches.' She giggled and went to get her tea.

When she came back she handed a parcel to her husband. 'I've been shopping today, darling. Picked up some of those shirts you like so much.'

'My sweet! how kind of you!' He began to tear at the brown paper like a schoolboy and produced three elegant shirts in cellophane covers. 'They're marvellous, my pet, you spoil me.' He looked up at me. 'Jim! These are the most wonderful shirts, you must have one.' He flicked a shinning package across the room on to my lap.

I looked down at it in amazement. 'No, really, I can't . . .'

'Of course you can. You keep it.'

'But Granville, not a shirt . . . it's too . . .'

'It's a very good shirt.' He was beginning to look hurt again.

I subsided.

They were both so kind. Zoe sat right by me with her tea cup, chatting pleasantly while Granville beamed at me from his chair as he finished the last of the sandwiches and started again on the onions.

The proximity of the attractive woman was agreeable but embarrassing. My corduroys in the warmth of the room had begun to give off the unmistakable bouquet of the farmyard where they spent most of their time. And though it was one of my favourite scents there was no doubt it didn't go with these elegant surroundings.

And worse still, I had started a series of internal rumblings and musical tinklings which resounded only too audibly during every lull in the conversation. The only other time I have heard such sounds was in a cow with an advanced case of displacement of the abomasum. My companions delicately feigned deafness even when I produced a shameful, explosive belch which made the little fat dog start up in alarm, but when another of these mighty borborygmi escaped me and almost made the windows rattle I thought it time to go.

In any case I wasn't contributing much else. The alcohol had taken hold and I was increasingly conscious that I was just sitting there with a stupid leer on my face. In striking contrast to Granville who looked just the same as when I first met him back at the surgery. He was cool and possessed, his massive urbanity unimpaired. It was a little hard.

So, with the tin of tobacco bumping against my hip and the shirt tucked under my arm I took my leave.

Back at the hospital I looked down at Dinah. The old dog had come through wonderfully well and she lifted her head and gazed at me sleepily. Her colour was good and her pulse strong. The operative shock had been dramatically minimised by my colleague's skilful speedy technique and by the intravenous drip.

I knelt down and stroked her ears. 'You know, I'm sure she's going to make it, Granville.'

Above me the great pipe nodded with majestic confidence.

'Of course, laddie, of course.'

And he was right. Dinah was rejuvenated by her hysterectomy and lived to delight her mistress for many more years.

On the way home that night she lay by my side on the passenger seat, her nose poking from a blanket. Now and then she rested her chin on my hand as it gripped the gear lever and occasionally she licked me lazily.

I could see she felt better than I did.

# Chapter 18

Ben Ashby the cattle dealer looked over the gate with his habitual deadpan expression. It always seemed to me that after a lifetime of buying cows from farmers he had developed a terror of showing any emotion which might be construed as enthusiasm. When he looked at a beast his face registered nothing beyond, occasionally, a gentle sorrow.

This was how it was this morning as he leaned on the top spar and directed a gloomy stare at Harry Sumner's heifer. After a few moments he turned to the farmer.

'I wish you'd had her in for me, Harry. She's too far away. I'm going to have to get over the top.' He began to climb stiffly upwards and it was then that he spotted Monty. The bull hadn't been so easy to see before as he cropped the grass among the group of heifers but suddenly the great head rose high above the others, the nose ring gleamed, and an ominous, strangled bellow sounded across the grass. And as he gazed at us he pulled absently at the turf with a fore foot.

Ben Ashby stopped climbing, hesitated for a second then returned to ground level.

'Aye well,' he muttered, still without changing expression. 'It's not that far away. I reckon I can see all right from here.'

Monty had changed a lot since the first day I saw him about two years ago. He had been a fortnight old then, a skinny, knock-kneed little creature, his head deep in a calf bucket.

'Well, what do you think of me new bull?' Harry Sumner had asked, laughing. 'Not much for a hundred quid is he?'

I whistled. 'As much as that?'

'Aye, it's a lot for a new-dropped calf, isn't it? But I can't think of any other way of getting into the Newton strain. I haven't the brass to buy a big 'un.'

Not all the farmers of those days were as far-seeing as Harry and some of them would use any type of male bovine to get their cows in calf.

One such man produced a gaunt animal for Siegfried's inspection and asked him what he thought of his bull. Siegfried's reply of 'All horns and balls' didn't please the owner but I still treasure it as the most graphic description of the typical scrub bull of that period.

Harry was a bright boy. He had inherited a little place of about a hundred acres on his father's death and with his young wife had set about making it go. He was in his early twenties and when I first saw him I had been deceived by his almost delicate appearance into thinking that he wouldn't be up to the job; the pallid face, the large, sensitive eyes and slender frame didn't seem fitted for the seven days a week milking, feeding, mucking-out slog that was dairy farming. But I had been wrong.

The fearless way he plunged in and grabbed at the hind feet of kicking cows for me to examine and his clenched-teeth determination as he hung on to the noses of the big loose beasts at testing time made me change my mind in a hurry. He worked endlessly and tirelessly and it was natural that his drive should have taken him to the south of Scotland to find a bull.

Harry's was an Ayrshire herd — unusual among the almost universal shorthorns in the Dales — and there was no doubt an injection of the famous Newton blood would be a sure way of improving his stock.

'He's got prize winners on both his sire and dam's side,' the young farmer said. 'And a grand pedigree name, too. Newton Montmorency the Sixth — Monty for short.'

As though recognising his name, the calf raised his head from the bucket and looked at us. It was a comic little face — wet-muzzled, milk slobbered half way up his cheeks and dribbling freely from his mouth. I bent over into the pen and scratched the top of the hard little head, feeling the tiny horn buds no bigger than peas under my fingers. Limpid-eyed and unafraid, Monty submitted calmly to the caress for a few moments then sank his head again in the bucket.

I saw quite a bit of Harry Sumner over

314

the next few weeks and usually had a look at his expensive purchase. And as the calf grew you could see why he had cost £100. He was in a pen with three of Harry's own calves and his superiority was evident at a glance; the broad forehead and wide-set eyes; the deep chest and short straight legs; the beautifully even line of the back from shoulder to tail head. Monty had class; and small as he was he was all bull.

He was about three months old when Harry rang to say he thought the calf had pneumonia. I was surprised because the weather was fine and warm and I knew Monty was in a draught-free building. But when I saw him I thought immediately that his owner's diagnosis was right. The heaving of the rib cage, the temperature of 105 degrees — it looked fairly straightforward. But when I got my stethoscope on his chest and listened for the pneumonic sounds I heard nothing. His lungs were perfectly clear. I went over him several times but there was not a squeak, not a rale, not the slightest sign of consolidation.

This was a facer. I turned to the

farmer. 'It's a funny one, Harry. He's sick, all right, but his symptoms don't add up to anything recognisable.'

I was going against my early training because the first vet I ever saw practice with in my student days told me once: 'If you don't know what's wrong with an animal for God's sake don't admit it. Give it a name — call it McLuskie's Disease or Galloping Dandruff — anything you like, but give it a name.' But no inspiration came to me. I looked at the panting, anxious-eyed little creature.

Treat the symptoms. That was the thing to do. He had a temperature so I'd try to get that down for a start. I brought out my pathetic armoury of febrifuges; the injection of non-specific antiserum, the 'fever drink' of sweet spirit of nitre; but over the next two days it was obvious that the time-honoured remedies were having no effect.

On the fourth morning, Harry Sumner met me as I got out of my car. 'He's walking funny, this morning, Mr Herriot — and he seems to be blind.'

'Blind!' An unusual form of lead-

316

poisoning — could that be it? I hurried into the calf pen and began to look round the walls, but there wasn't a scrap of paint anywhere and Monty had spent his entire life in there.

And anyway, as I looked at him I realised that he wasn't really blind; his eyes were staring and slightly upturned and he blundered unseeingly around the pen, but he blinked as I passed my hand in front of his face. To complete my bewilderment he walked with a wooden, stiff-legged gait almost like a mechanical toy and my mind began to snatch at diagnostic straws — tetanus, no — meningitis — no, no; I always tried to maintain the calm, professional exterior but I had to fight an impulse to scratch my head and stand gaping.

I got off the place as quickly as possible and settled down to serious thought as I drove away. My lack of experience didn't help, but I did have a knowledge of pathology and physiology and when stumped for a diagnosis I could usually work something out on rational grounds. But this thing didn't make sense.

That night I got out my books, notes from college, back numbers of the Veterinary Record and anything else I could find on the subject of calf diseases. Somewhere here there would surely be a clue. But the volumes on medicine and surgery were barren of inspiration and I had about given up hope when I came upon the passage in a little pamphlet on calf diseases. 'Peculiar, stilted gait, staring eyes with a tendency to gaze upwards, occasionally respiratory symptoms with high temperature.' The words seemed to leap out at me from the printed page and it was as though the unknown author was patting me on the shoulder and murmuring reassuringly: 'This is it, you see. It's all perfectly clear.'

I grabbed the phone and rang Harry Sumner. 'Harry, have you ever noticed Monty and those other calves in the pen licking each other?'

'Aye, they're allus at it, the little beggars. It's like a hobby with them. Why?'

'Well I know what's wrong with your

bull. He's got a hair ball.'

'A hair ball? Where?'

'In the abomasum — the fourth stomach. That's what's setting up all those strange symptoms.'

'Well I'll go to hell. What do we do about it, then?'

'It'll probably mean an operation, but I'd like to try dosing him with liquid paraffin first. I'll put a pint bottle on the step for you if you'll come and collect it. Give him a half a pint now and the same first thing in the morning. It might just grease the thing through. I'll see you tomorrow.'

I hadn't a lot of faith in the liquid paraffin. I suppose I suggested it for the sake of doing something while I played nervously with the idea of operating. And next morning the picture was as I expected; Monty was still rigid-limbed, still staring sightlessly ahead of him, and an oiliness round his rectum and down his tail showed that the paraffin had by-passed the obstruction.

'He hasn't had a bite now for three days,' Harry said. 'I doubt he won't stick it much longer.'

I looked from his worried face to the little animal trembling in the pen. 'You're right. We'll have to open him up straight away to have any hope of saving him. Are you willing to let me have a go?'

'Oh aye, let's be at t'job — sooner the better.' He smiled at me. It was a confident smile and my stomach gave a lurch. His confidence could be badly misplaced because in those days abdominal surgery in the bovine was in a primitive state. There were a few jobs we had begun to tackle fairly regularly but removal of a hair ball wasn't one of them and my knowledge of the procedure was confined to some rather small-print reading in the text books.

But this young farmer had faith in me. He thought I could do the job so it was no good letting him see my doubts. It was at times like this that I envied our colleagues in human medicine. When a surgical case came up they packed their patient off to a hospital but the vet just had to get his jacket off on the spot and make an operating theatre out of the farm buildings.

Harry and I busied ourselves in boiling up the instruments, setting out buckets of hot water and laying a clean bed of straw in an empty pen. Despite his weakness the calf took nearly sixty c.c.'s of Nembutal into his vein before he was fully anaesthetised but finally he was asleep, propped on his back between two straw bales, his little hooves dangling above him. I was ready to start.

It's never the same as it is in the books. The pictures and diagrams look so simple and straightforward but it is a different thing when you are cutting into a living, breathing creature with the abdomen rising and falling gently and the blood oozing beneath your knife. The abomasum, I knew, was just down there, slightly to the right of the sternum but as I cut through the peritoneum there was this slippery mass of fat-streaked omentum obscuring everything; and as I pushed it aside one of the bales moved and Monty tilted to his left causing a sudden gush of intestines into the wound. I put the flat of my hand against the shining pink loops —

it would be just great if my patient's insides started spilling out on to the straw before I had started.

'Pull him upright, Harry, and shove that bale back into place,' I gasped. The farmer quickly complied but the intestines weren't at all anxious to return to their place and kept intruding coyly as I groped for the abomasum. Frankly I was beginning to feel just a bit lost and my heart was thudding when I came upon something hard. It was sliding about beyond the wall of one of the stomachs — at the moment I wasn't sure which. I gripped it and lifted it into the wound. I had hold of the abomasum and that hard thing inside must be the hair ball.

Repelling the intestines which had made another determined attempt to push their way into the act, I incised the stomach and had my first look at the cause of the trouble. It wasn't a ball at all, rather a flat plaque of densely matted hair mixed freely with strands of hay, sour curd and a shining covering of my liquid paraffin. The whole thing was jammed against the pyloric opening.

Gingerly I drew it out through the incision and dropped it in the straw. It wasn't till I had closed the stomach wound with the gut, stitched up the muscle layer and had started on the skin that I realised that the sweat was running down my face. As I blew away a droplet from my nose end Harry broke the silence.

'It's a hell of a tricky job, isn't it?' he said. Then he laughed and thumped my shoulder. 'I bet you felt a bit queer the first time you did one of these!'

I pulled another strand of suture silk through and knotted it. 'You're right, Harry.' I said. 'How right you are.'

When I had finished we covered Monty with a horse rug and piled straw on top of that, leaving only his head sticking out. I bent over and touched a corner of the eye. Not a vestige of a corneal reflex. God, he was deep — had I given him too much anaesthetic? And of course there'd be surgical shock, too. As I left I glanced back at the motionless little animal. He looked smaller than ever and very vulnerable under the bare walls of the pen.

I was busy for the rest of the day but that evening my thoughts kept coming back to Monty. Had he come out of it yet? Maybe he was dead. I hadn't the experience of previous cases to guide me and I simply had no idea of how a calf reacted to an operation like that. And I couldn't rid myself of the nagging consciousness of how much it all meant to Harry Sumner. The bull is half the herd, they say, and half of Harry's future herd was lying there under the straw — he wouldn't be able to find that much money again.

I jumped suddenly from my chair. It was no good, I had to find out what was happening. Part of me rebelled at the idea of looking amateurish and unsure of myself by going fussing back, but, I thought, I could always say I had returned to look for an instrument.

The farm was in darkness as I crept into the pen. I shone my torch on the mound of straw and saw with a quick bump of the heart that the calf had not moved. I dropped to my knees and pushed a hand under the rug; he was breathing anyway.

324

But there was still no eye reflex — either he was dying or he was taking a hell of a time to come out.

In the shadows of the yard I looked across at the soft glow from the farmhouse kitchen. Nobody had heard me. I slunk over to the car and drove off with the sick knowledge that I was no further forward. I still didn't know how the job was going to turn out.

Next morning I had to go through the same thing again and as I walked stiffly across to the calf pen I knew for sure I'd see something this time. Either he'd be dead or better. I opened the outer door and almost ran down the passage. It was the third pen along and I stared hungrily into it.

Monty was sitting up on his chest. He was still under the rug and straw and he looked sorry for himself but when a bovine animal is on its chest I always feel hopeful. The tensions flowed from me in a great wave. He had survived the operation — the first stage was over; and as I knelt rubbing the top of his head I had the feeling that we were going to win.

And, in fact, he did get better, though I have always found it difficult to explain to myself scientifically why the removal of that pad of tangled fibres could cause such a dramatic improvement in so many directions. But there it was. His temperature did drop and his breathing returned to normal, his eyes did stop staring and the weird stiffness disappeared from his limbs.

But though I couldn't understand it, I was none the less delighted. Like a teacher with his favourite pupil I developed a warm proprietary affection for the calf and when I happened to be on the farm I found my feet straying unbidden to his pen. He always walked up to me and regarded me with friendly interest; it was as if he had a fellow feeling for me, too.

He was rather more than a year old when I noticed the change. The friendly interest gradually disappeared from his eyes and was replaced by a thoughtful, speculative look; and he developed a habit of shaking his head at me at the same time.

'I'd stop going in there, Mr Herriot, if I were you,' Harry said one day. 'He's getting big and I reckon he's going to be a cheeky bugger before he's finished.'

But cheeky was the wrong word. Harry had a long, trouble-free spell and Monty was nearly two years old when I saw him again. It wasn't a case of illness this time. One or two of Harry's cows had been calving before their time and it was typical of him that he should ask me to blood test his entire herd for Brucellosis.

We worked our way easily through the cows and I had a long row of glass tubes filled with blood in just over an hour.

'Well, that's the lot in here,' the farmer said. 'We only have bull to do and we're finished.' He led the way across the yard through the door into the calf pens and along a passage to the bull box at the end. He opened the half door and as I looked inside I felt a sudden sense of shock.

Monty was enormous. The neck with its jutting humps of muscle supported a head so huge that the eyes looked tiny. And there was nothing friendly in those eyes now; no expression at all, in fact, only a cold black glitter. He was standing sideways to me, facing the wall, but I knew he was watching me as he pushed his head against the stones, his great horns scoring the whitewash with slow, menacing deliberation. Occasionally he snorted from deep in his chest but apart from that he remained ominously still. Monty wasn't just a bull — he was a vast, brooding presence.

Harry grinned as he saw me staring over the door. 'Well, do you fancy popping inside to scratch his head? That's what you allus used to do.'

'No thanks.' I dragged my eyes away from the animal. 'But I wonder what my expectation of life would be if I did go in.'

'I reckon you'd last about a minute,' Harry said thoughtfully. 'He's a grand bull — all I ever expected — but by God he's a mean 'un. I never trust him an inch.'

'And how,' I asked without enthusiasm, 'am I supposed to get a sample of blood from him?'

'Oh I'll trap his head in yon corner.' Harry pointed to a metal yoke above a trough in an opening into the yard at the far side of the box. 'I'll give him some meal to 'tice him in.' He went back down the passage and soon I could see him out in the yard scooping meal into the trough.

The bull at first took no notice and continued to prod at the wall with his horns, then he turned with awesome slowness, took a few unhurried steps across the box and put his nose down to the trough. Harry, out of sight in the yard, pulled the lever and the yoke crashed shut on the great neck.

'All right,' the farmer cried, hanging on to the lever, 'I have 'im. You can go in now.'

I opened the door and entered the box and though the bull was held fast by the head there was still the uneasy awareness that he and I were alone in that small space together. And as I passed along the massive body and put my hand on the neck I sensed a quivering emanation of pent up power and rage. Digging my fingers into the jugular furrow I watched the vein rise up and poised my needle. It would take a good hard thrust to pierce that leathery skin.

The bull stiffened but did not move as I plunged the needle in and with relief I saw the blood flowing darkly into the syringe. Thank God I had hit the vein first time and didn't have to start poking around. I was withdrawing the needle and thinking that the job had been so simple after all when everything started to happen. The bull gave a tremendous bellow and whipped round at me with no trace of his former lethargy. I saw that he had got one horn out of the yoke and though he couldn't reach me with his head his shoulder knocked me on my back with a terrifying revelation of unbelievable strength. I heard Harry shouting from outside and as I scrambled up and headed for the box door I saw that the madly plunging creature had almost got his second horn clear and when I reached the passage I heard the clang of the yoke as he finally freed himself.

Anybody who has travelled a narrow passage a few feet ahead of about a ton of snorting, pounding death will appreciate that I didn't dawdle. I was spurred on by the certain knowledge that if Monty caught me he would plaster me against the wall as effortlessly as I would squash a ripe plum, and though I was clad in a long oilskin coat and wellingtons I doubt whether an olympic sprinter in full running kit would have bettered my time.

I made the door at the end with a foot to spare, dived through and crashed it shut. The first thing I saw was Harry Sumner running round from the outside of the box. He was very pale. I couldn't see my face but it felt pale; even my lips were cold and numb.

'God, I'm sorry!' Harry said hoarsely. 'The yoke couldn't have closed properly — that bloody great neck of his. The lever just jerked out of my hand. Damn, I'm glad to see you — I thought you were a goner!'

I looked down at my hand. The blood-filled syringe was still tightly clutched there. 'Well I've got my sample anyway, Harry. And it's just as well, because it would take some fast talking to get me in there to try for another. I'm afraid you've just seen the end of a beautiful friendship.'

'Aye, the big sod!' Harry listened for a few moments to the thudding of Monty's horns against the door. 'And after all you did for him. That's gratitude for you.'

# Chapter 19

Probably the most dramatic occurrence in the history of veterinary practice was the disappearance of the draught horse. It is an almost incredible fact that this glory and mainstay of the profession just melted quietly away within a few years. And I was one of those who were there to see it happen.

When I first came to Darrowby the tractor had already begun to take over, but tradition dies hard in the agricultural world and there were still a lot of horses around. Which was just as well because my veterinary education had been geared to things equine with everything else a poor second. It had been a good scientific education in many respects but at times I wondered if the people who designed it still had a mental picture of the horse doctor with his top hat and frock coat busying himself in a world of horse-drawn trams and brewers' drays.

We learned the anatomy of the horse in great detail, then that of the other animals much more superficially. It was the same with the other subjects; from animal husbandry with such insistence on a thorough knowledge of shoeing that we developed into amateur blacksmiths — right up to medicine and surgery where it was much more important to know about glanders and strangles than canine distemper. Even as we were learning, we youngsters knew it was ridiculous, with the draught horse already cast as a museum piece and the obvious potential of cattle and small animal work.

Still, as I say, after we had absorbed a vast store of equine lore it was a certain comfort that there were still a lot of patients on which we could try it out. I should think in my first two years I treated farm horses nearly every day and though I never was and never will be an equine expert there was a strange thrill in meeting with the age-old conditions whose names rang down almost from mediaeval times. Quittor, fistulous withers, poll evil, thrush, shoulder slip — vets had been wrestling with them for hundreds of years using very much the same drugs and procedures as myself. Armed with my firing iron and box of blister I plunged determinedly into what had always been the surging mainstream of veterinary life.

And now, in less than three years the stream had dwindled, not exactly to a trickle but certainly to the stage where the final dry-up was in sight. This meant, in a way, a lessening of the pressures on the veterinary surgeon because there is no doubt that horse work was the roughest and most arduous part of our life.

So that today, as I looked at the three year old gelding it occurred to me that this sort of thing wasn't happening as often as it did. He had a long tear in his flank where he had caught himself on barbed wire and it gaped open whenever he moved. There was no getting away from the fact that it had to be stitched.

The horse was tied by the head in his stall, his right side against the tall wooden partition. One of the farm men, a hefty six footer, took a tight hold of the head collar and leaned back against the manger as I puffed some iodoform into the wound. The horse didn't seem to mind, which was a comfort because he was a massive animal emanating an almost tangible vitality and power. I threaded my needle with a length of silk, lifted one of the lips of the wound and passed it through. This was going to be no trouble, I thought as I lifted the flap at the other side and pierced it, but as I was drawing the needle through, the gelding made a convulsive leap and I felt as though a great wind had whistled across the front of my body. Then, strangely, he was standing there against the wooden boards as if nothing had happened.

On the occasions when I have been kicked I have never seen it coming. It is surprising how quickly those great muscular legs can whip out. But there was no doubt he had had a good go at me because my needle and silk were nowhere to be seen, the big man at the head was staring at me with wide eyes in a chalk white face and the front of my clothing was in an extraordinary state. I was wearing a 'gaberdine mac' and it looked as if somebody had taken a razor blade and painstakingly cut the material into narrow strips which hung down in ragged strips to ground level. The great iron-shod hoof had missed my legs by an inch or two but my mac was a write-off.

I was standing there looking around me in a kind of stupor when I heard a cheerful hail from the doorway.

'Now then, Mr Herriot, what's he done at you?' Cliff Tyreman, the old horseman, looked me up and down with a mixture of amusement and asperity.

'He's nearly put me in hospital, Cliff,' I replied shakily. 'About the closest near miss I've ever had. I just felt the wind of it.'

'What were you tryin' to do?'

'Stitch that wound, but I'm not going to try any more. I'm off to the surgery to get a chloroform muzzle.'

The little man looked shocked. 'You don't need no chloroform. I'll haul him and you'll have no trouble.'

'I'm sorry, Cliff.' I began to put away

my suture materials, scissors and powder. 'You're a good bloke, I know, but he's had one go at me and he's not getting another chance. I don't want to be lame for the rest of my life.'

The horseman's small, wiry frame seemed to bunch into a ball of aggression. He thrust forward his head in a characteristic posture and glared at me. 'I've never heard owt as daft in me life.' Then he swung round on the big man who was still hanging on to the horse's head, the ghastly pallor of his face now tinged with a delicate green. 'Come on out o' there, Bob! You're that bloody scared you're upsetting t'oss. Come on out of it and let me have 'im!'

Bob gratefully left the head and, grinning sheepishly moved with care along the side of the horse. He passed Cliff on the way and the little man's head didn't reach his shoulder.

Cliff seemed thoroughly insulted by the whole business. He took hold of the head collar and regarded the big animal with the disapproving stare of a schoolmaster at a naughty child. The horse, still in the mood for trouble, laid back his ears and began to plunge about the stall, his huge feet clattering ominously on the stone floor, but he came to rest quickly as the little man uppercutted him furiously in the ribs.

'Get stood up straight there, ye big bugger. What's the matter with ye?' Cliff barked and again he planted his tiny fist against the swelling barrel of the chest, a puny blow which the animal could scarcely have felt but which reduced him to quivering submission. 'Try to kick, would you, eh? I'll bloody fettle you!' He shook the head collar and fixed the horse with a hypnotic stare as he spoke. Then he turned to me. 'You can come and do your job, Mr Herriot, he won't hurt tha.'

I looked irresolutely at the huge, lethal animal. Stepping open-eyed into dangerous situations is something vets are called upon regularly to do and I suppose we all react differently. I know there were times when an over-vivid imagination made me acutely aware of the dire possibilities and now my mind seemed to be dwelling voluptuously on the frightful power in those enormous shining quarters, on the unyielding flintiness of the spatulate feet with their rim of metal. Cliff's voice cut into my musings.

'Come on, Mr Herriot, I tell ye he won't hurt tha.'

I reopened my box and tremblingly threaded another needle. I didn't seem to have much option; the little man wasn't asking me, he was telling me. I'd have to try again.

I couldn't have been a very impressive sight as I shuffled forwards, almost tripping over the tattered hula-hula skirt which dangled in front of me, my shaking hands reaching out once more for the wound, my heart thundering in my ears. But I needn't have worried. It was just as the little man had said; he didn't hurt me. In fact he never moved. He seemed to be listening attentively to the muttering which Cliff was directing into his face from a few inches' range. I powdered and stitched and clipped as though working on an anatomical specimen. Chloroform couldn't have done it any better.

As I retreated thankfully from the stall

and began again to put away my instruments the monologue at the horse's head began to change its character. The menacing growl was replaced by a wheedling, teasing chuckle.

'Well, ye see, you're just a daft awd bugger, getting yourself all airigated over nowt. You're a good lad, really, aren't ye, a real good lad.' Cliff's hand ran caressingly over the neck and the towering animal began to nuzzle his cheek, as completely in his sway as any Labrador puppy.

When he had finished he came slowly from the stall, stroking the back, ribs, belly and quarters, even giving a playful tweak at the tail on parting while what had been a few minutes ago an explosive mountain of bone and muscle submitted happily.

I pulled a packet of Gold Flake from my pocket. 'Cliff, you're a marvel. Will you have a cigarette?'

'It 'ud be like givin' a pig a strawberry,' the little man replied, then he thrust forth his tonque on which reposed a half-chewed gobbet of tobacco. 'It's allus there. Ah push it in fust thing every mornin' soon as I get out of bed and there it stays. You'd never know, would you?'

I must have looked comically surprised because the dark eyes gleamed and the rugged little face split into a delighted grin. I looked at that grin — boyish, invincible — and reflected on the phenomenon that was Cliff Tyreman.

In a community in which toughness and durability was the norm he stood out as something exceptional. When I had first seen him nearly three years ago barging among cattle, grabbing their noses and hanging on effortlessly, I had put him down as an unusually fit middle-aged man; but he was in fact nearly seventy. There wasn't much of him but he was formidable; with his long arms swinging, his stumping, pigeon-toed gait and his lowered head he seemed always to be butting his way through life.

'I didn't expect to see you today,' I said. 'I heard you had pneumonia.'

He shrugged. 'Aye, summat of t'sort. First time I've ever been off work since I was a lad.'

'And you should be in your bed now, I should say.' I looked at the heaving chest and partly open mouth. 'I could hear you wheezing away when you were at the horse's head.'

'Nay, I can't stick that nohow. I'll be right in a day or two.' He seized a shovel and began busily clearing away the heap of manure behind the horse, his breathing loud and sterterous in the silence.

Harland Grange was a large, mainly arable farm in the low country at the foot of the Dale, and there had been a time when this stable had had a horse standing in every one of the long row of stalls. There had been over twenty with at least twelve regularly at work, but now there were only two, the young horse I had been treating and an ancient grey called Badger.

Cliff had been head horseman and when the revolution came he turned to tractoring and other jobs around the farm with no fuss at all. This was typical of the reaction of thousands of other farm workers throughout the country; they didn't set up a howl at having to abandon the skills of a lifetime and start anew — they just got on with it. In fact, the younger men seized avidly upon the new machines and proved themselves natural mechanics.

But to the old experts like Cliff, something had gone. He would say: 'It's a bloody sight easier sitting on a tractor — it used to play 'ell with me feet walking up and down them fields all day.' But he couldn't lose his love of horses; the fellow feeling between working man and working beast which had grown in him since childhood and was in his blood forever.

My next visit to the farm was to see a fat bullock with a piece of turnip stuck in his throat but while I was there, the farmer, Mr Gilling, asked me to have a look at old Badger.

'He's had a bit of a cough lately. Maybe it's just his age, but see what you think.'

The old horse was the sole occupant of the stable now. 'I've sold the three year old,' Mr Gilling said. 'But I'll still keep the old 'un — he'll be useful for a bit of light carting.'

I glanced sideways at the farmer's granite features. He looked the least sentimental of men but I knew why he was keeping the old horse. It was for Cliff.

'Cliff will be pleased, anyway,' I said.

Mr Gilling nodded. 'Aye, I never knew such a feller for 'osses. He was never happier than when he was with them.' He gave a short laugh. 'Do you know, I can remember years ago when he used to fall out with his missus he'd come down to this stable of a night and sit among his 'osses. Just sit here for hours on end looking at 'em and smoking. That was before he started chewing tobacco.'

'And did you have Badger in those days?'

'Aye, we bred him. Cliff helped at his foaling — I remember the little beggar came arse first and we had a bit of a job pullin' him out.' He smiled again. 'Maybe that's why he was always Cliff's favourite. He always worked Badger himself — year in year out — and he was that proud of 'im that if he had to take him into the town for any reason he'd plait ribbons into his mane and hang all his brasses on him first.' He shook his head reminiscently.

The old horse looked round with mild interest as I went up to him. He was in his late twenties and everything about him suggested serene old age; the gaunt projection of the pelvic bones, the whiteness of face and muzzle, the sunken eye with its benign expression. As I was about to take his temperature he gave a sharp, barking cough and it gave me the first clue to his ailment. I watched the rise and fall of his breathing for a minute or two and the second clue was there to be seen; further examination was unnecessary.

'He's broken winded, Mr Gilling,' I said. 'Or he's got pulmonary emphysema to give it its proper name. Do you see that double lift of the abdomen as he breathes out? That's because his lungs have lost their elasticity and need an extra effort to force the air out.'

'What's caused it, then?'

'Well it's to do with his age, but he's got a bit of cold on him at the moment and that's brought it out.'

'Will he get rid of it in time?' the farmer asked.

'He'll be a bit better when he gets over his cold, but I'm afraid he'll never be quite right. I'll give you some medicine to put in his drinking water which will alleviate his symptoms.' I went out to the car for a bottle of the arsenical expectorant mixture which we used then.

It was about six weeks later that I heard from Mr Gilling again. He rang me about seven o'clock one evening.

'I'd like you to come out and have a look at old Badger,' he said.

'What's wrong? Is it his broken wind again?'

'No, it's not that. He's still got the cough but it doesn't seem to bother him much. No, I think he's got a touch of colic. I've got to go out but Cliff will attend to you.'

The little man was waiting for me in the yard. He was carrying an oil lamp. As I came up to him I exclaimed in horror.

'Good God, Cliff, what have you been doing to yourself?' His face was a patchwork of cuts and scratches and his nose, almost without skin, jutted from

347

between two black eyes.

He grinned through the wounds, his eyes dancing with merriment. 'Came off me bike 'tother day. Hit a stone and went right over handlebars, arse over tip.' He burst out laughing at the very thought.

'But damn it, man, haven't you been to a doctor? You're not fit to be out in that state.'

'Doctor? Nay, there's no need to bother them fellers. It's nowt much.' He fingered a gash on his jaw. 'Ah lapped me chin up for a day in a bit o' bandage, but it's right enough now.'

I shook my head as I followed him into the stable. He hung up the oil lamp then went over to the horse.

'Can't reckon t'awd feller up,' he said. 'You'd think there wasn't much ailing him but there's summat.'

There were no signs of violent pain but the animal kept transferring his weight from one hind foot to the other as if he did have a little abdominal discomfort. His temperature was normal and he didn't show symptoms of anything else.

I looked at him doubtfully. 'Maybe he

has a bit of colic. There's nothing else to see, anyway. I'll give him an injection to settle him down.'

'Right you are, maister, that's good.' Cliff watched me get my syringe out then he looked around him into the shadows at the far end of the stable.

'Funny seeing only one 'oss standing here. I remember when there was a great long row of 'em and the barfins and bridles hangin' there on the stalls and the rest of the harness behind them all shinin' on t'wall.' He transferred his plug of tobacco to the other side of his mouth and smiled. 'By gaw, I were in here at six o'clock every morning feedin' them and gettin' them ready for work and ah'll tell you it was a sight to see us all goin' off ploughing at the start o' the day. Maybe six pairs of 'osses setting off with their harness jinglin' and the ploughmen sittin' sideways on their backs. Like a regular procession it was.'

I smiled. 'It was an early start, Cliff.'

'Aye, by Gaw, and a late finish. We'd bring the 'osses home at night and give 'em a light feed and take their harness off, then we'd go and have our own teas and we'd be back 'ere again afterwards, curry-combing and dandy-brushin' all the sweat and dirt off 'em. Then we'd give them a right good stiff feed of chop and oats and hay to set 'em up for the next day.'

'There wouldn't be much left of the evening then, was there?'

'Nay, there wasn't. It was about like work and bed, I reckon, but it never bothered us.'

I stepped forward to give Badger the injection, then paused. The old horse had undergone a slight spasm, a barely perceptible stiffening of the muscles, and as I looked at him he cocked his tail for a second then lowered it.

'There's something else here,' I said. 'Will you bring him out of his stall, Cliff, and let me see him walk across the yard.'

And watching him clop over the cobbles I saw it again; the stiffness, the raising of the tail. Something clicked in my mind. I walked over and rapped him under the chin and as the membrana nictitans flicked across his eye then slid slowly back I knew.

I paused for a moment. My casual little visit had suddenly become charged with doom.

'Cliff,' I said. 'I'm afraid he's got tetanus.'

'Lockjaw, you mean?'

'That's right. I'm sorry, but there's no doubt about it. Has he had any wounds lately — especially in his feet?'

'Well he were dead lame about a fortnight ago and blacksmith let some matter out of his hoof. Made a right big 'ole.'

There it was. 'It's a pity he didn't get an anti-tetanus shot at the time,' I said. I put my hand into the animal's mouth and tried to prise it open but the jaws were clamped tightly together. 'I don't suppose he's been able to eat today.'

'He had a bit this morning but nowt tonight. What's the lookout for him, Mr Herriot?'

What indeed? If Cliff had asked me the same question today I would have been just as troubled to give him an answer. The facts are that seventy to eighty per cent of tetanus cases die and whatever you do to them in the way of treatment doesn't seem to make a whit of difference to those figures. But I didn't want to sound entirely defeatist.

'It's a very serious condition as you know, Cliff, but I'll do all I can. I've got some antitoxin in the car and I'll inject that into his vein and if the spasms get very bad I'll give him a sedative. As long as he can drink there's a chance for him because he'll have to live on fluids — gruel would be fine.'

For a few days Badger didn't get any worse and I began to hope. I've seen tetanus horses recover and it is a wonderful experience to come in one day and find that the jaws have relaxed and the hungry animal can once more draw food into its mouth.

But it didn't happen with Badger. They had got the old horse into a big loose box where he could move around in comfort and each day as I looked over the half door I felt myself willing him to show some little sign of improvement; but instead, after that first few days he began to deteriorate. A sudden movement or the approach of any person would throw him into a violent spasm so that he would stagger stiff-legged round the box like a big wooden toy, his eyes terrified, saliva drooling from between his fiercely clenched teeth. One morning I was sure he would fall and I suggested putting him in slings. I had to go back to the surgery for the slings and it was just as I was entering Skeldale House that the phone rang.

It was Mr Gilling. 'He's beat us to it, I'm afraid. He's flat out on the floor and I doubt it's a bad job, Mr Herriot. We'll have to put him down, won't we?'

'I'm afraid so.'

'There's just one thing. Mallock will be taking him away but old Cliff says he doesn't want Mallock to shoot 'im. Wants you to do it. Will you come?'

I got out the humane killer and drove back to the farm, wondering at the fact that the old man should find the idea of my bullet less repugnant than the knacker man's. Mr Gilling was waiting in the box and by his side Cliff, shoulders hunched, hands deep in his pockets. He turned to me with a strange smile.

'I was just saying to t'boss how grand t'awd lad used to look when I got 'im up for a show. By Gaw you should have seen him with 'is coat polished and the feathers on his legs scrubbed as white as snow and a big blue ribbon round his tail.'

'I can imagine it, Cliff,' I said. 'Nobody could have looked after him better.'

He took his hands from his pockets, crouched by the prostrate animal and for a few minutes stroked the white-flecked neck and pulled at the ears while the old sunken eye looked at him impassively.

He began to speak softly to the old horse but his voice was steady, almost conversational, as though he was chatting to a friend.

'Many's the thousand miles I've walked after you, awd lad, and many's the talk we've had together. But I didn't have to say much to tha, did I? I reckon you knew every move I made, everything I said. Just one little word and you always did what ah wanted you to do.'

He rose to his feet. 'I'll get on with me work now, boss,' he said firmly, and strode out of the box.

I waited awhile so that he would not hear the bang which signaled the end of Badger, the end of the horses of Harland Grange and the end of the sweet core of Cliff Tyreman's life.

As I was leaving I saw the little man again. He was mounting the iron seat of a roaring tractor and I shouted to him above the noise.

'The boss says he's going to get some sheep in and you'll be doing a bit of shepherding. I think you'll enjoy that.'

Cliff's undefeated grin flashed out as he called back to me.

'Aye, I don't mind learnin' summat new. I'm nobbut a lad yet!

# Chapter 20

This was a different kind of ringing. I had gone to sleep as the great bells in the church tower down the street pealed for the Christmas midnight mass, but this was a sharper, shriller sound.

It was difficult at first to shake off the mantle of unreality in which I had wrapped myself last night. Last night — Christmas Eve. It had been like a culmination of all the ideas I had ever held about Christmas — a flowering of emotions I had never experienced before. It had been growing in me since the afternoon call to a tiny village where the snow lay deep on the single street and on the walls and on the ledges of the windows where the lights on the tinseled trees glowed red and blue and gold; and as I left it in the dusk I drove beneath the laden branches of a group of dark spruce as motionless as though they had been sketched against the white background of the fields. And when I reached Darrowby it was dark and around the market place the little shops were bright with decorations and the light from their windows fell in a soft yellow wash over the trodden snow of the cobbles. People, anonymously muffled, were hurrying about, doing their last minute shopping, their feet slithering over the rounded stones.

I had known many Christmases in Scotland but they had taken second place to the New Year celebrations; there had been none of this air of subdued excitement which started days before with folks shouting good wishes and coloured lights winking on the lonely fellsides and the farmers' wives plucking the fat geese, the feathers piled deep around their feet. And for fully two weeks you heard the children piping carols in the street then knocking on the door for sixpences. And best of all, last night the methodist choir had sung out there, filling the night air with rich, thrilling harmony.

Before going to bed and just as the

church bells began I closed the door of Skeldale House behind me and walked again into the market place. Nothing stirred now in the white square stretching smooth and cold and empty under the moon, and there was a Dickens look about the ring of houses and shops put together long before anybody thought of town planning; tall and short, fat and thin, squashed in crazily around the cobbles, their snow-burdened roofs jagged and uneven against the frosty sky.

As I walked back, the snow crunching under my feet, the bells clanging, the sharp air tingling in my nostrils, the wonder and mystery of Christmas enveloped me in a great wave. Peace on earth, goodwill towards men; the words became meaningful as never before and I saw myself suddenly as a tiny particle in the scheme of things; Darrowby, the farmers, the animals and me seemed for the first time like a warm, comfortable entity. I hadn't been drinking but I almost floated up the stairs to our bed-sitter.

Helen was still asleep and as I crawled between the sheets beside her I was still wallowing in my Yuletide euphoria. There wouldn't be much work tomorrow; we'd have a long lie — maybe till nine — and then a lazy day, a glorious hiatus in our busy life. As I drifted into sleep it was as though I was surrounded by the smiling faces of my clients looking down at me with an all-embracing benevolence; and strangely I fancied I could hear singing, sweet and haunting, just like the methodist choir — God Rest Ye Merry Gentlemen . . .

But now there was this other bell which wouldn't stop. Must be the alarm. But as I pawed at the clock the noise continued and I saw that it was six o'clock. It was the phone of course. I lifted the receiver.

A metallic voice, crisp and very wide awake, jarred in my ear. 'Is that the vet?'

'Yes, Herriot speaking,' I mumbled.

'This is Brown, Willet Hill. I've got a cow down with milk fever. I want you here quick.'

'Right, I'll see to it.'

'Don't take ower long.' Then a click at the far end.

I rolled on to my back and stared at the

ceiling. So this was Christmas Day. The day when I was going to step out of the world for a spell and luxuriate in the seasonal spirit. I hadn't bargained for this fellow jerking me brutally back to reality. And not a word of regret or apology. No 'sorry to get you out of bed' or anything else, never mind 'Merry Christmas.' It was just a bit hard.

Mr Brown was waiting for me in the darkness of the farmyard. I had been to his place a few times before and as my headlights blazed on him I was struck, as always, by his appearance of perfect physical fitness. He was a gingery man of about forty with high cheekbones set in a sharp-featured clear-skinned face. Red hair peeped from under a check cap and a faint auburn down covered his cheeks, his neck, the backs of his hands. It made me feel a bit more sleepy just to look at him.

He didn't say good morning but nodded briefly then jerked his head in the direction of the byre. 'She's in there' was all he said.

He watched in silence as I gave the injections and it wasn't until I was putting the empty bottles into my pocket that he spoke.

'Don't suppose I'll have to milk her today?'

'No,' I replied. 'Better leave the bag full.'

'Anything special about feedin'?'

'No, she can have anything she likes when she wants it.' Mr Brown was very efficient. Always wanted to know every detail.

As we crossed the yard he halted suddenly and turned to face me. Could it be that he was going to ask me in for a nice hot cup of tea?

'You know,' he said, as I stood ankle deep in the snow, the frosty air nipping at my ears. 'I've had a few of these cases lately. Maybe there's summat wrong with my routine. Do you think I'm steaming up my cows too much?'

'It's quite possible.' I hurried towards the car. One thing I wasn't going to do was deliver a lecture on animal husbandry at this moment.

My hand was on the door handle when he said 'I'll give you another ring if she's not up by dinner time. And there's one other thing — that was a hell of a bill I had from you fellers last month, so tell your boss not to be so savage with 'is pen.' Then he turned and walked quickly towards the house.

Well that was nice, I thought as I drove away. Not even thanks or goodbye, just a complaint and a promise to haul me away from my roast goose if necessary. A sudden wave of anger surged in me. Bloody farmers! There were some miserable devils among them. Mr Brown had doused my festive feeling as effectively as if he had thrown a bucket of water over me.

As I mounted the steps of Skeldale House the darkness had paled to a shivery grey. Helen met me in the passage. She was carrying a tray.

'I'm sorry, Jim,' she said. 'There's another urgent job. Siegfried's had to go out, too. But I've got a cup of coffee and some fried bread for you. Come in and sit down — you've got time to eat it before you go.'

I sighed. It was going to be just another

day after all. 'What's this about, Helen?' I asked, sipping the coffee.

'It's old Mr Kirby,' she replied. 'He's very worried about his nanny goat.'

'Nanny goat!'

'Yes, he says she's choking.'

'Choking! How the heck can she be choking?' I shouted.

'I really don't know. And I wish you wouldn't shout at me, Jim. It's not my fault.'

In an instant I was engulfed by shame. Here I was, in a bad temper, taking it out on my wife. It is a common reaction for vets to blame the hapless person who passes on an unwanted message but I am not proud of it. I held out my hand and Helen took it.

'I'm sorry,' I said and finished the coffee sheepishly. My feeling of goodwill was at a very low ebb.

Mr Kirby was a retired farmer, but he had sensibly taken a cottage with a bit of land where he kept enough stock to occupy his time — a cow, a few pigs and his beloved goats. He had always had goats, even when he was running his dairy herd;

he had a thing about them.

The cottage was in a village high up the Dale. Mr Kirby met me at the gate.

'Ee, lad,' he said. 'I'm right sorry to be bothering you this early in the morning and Christmas an' all, but I didn't have no choice. Dorothy's real bad.'

He led the way to a stone shed which had been converted into a row of pens. Behind the wire of one of them a large white Saanen goat peered out at us anxiously and as I watched her she gulped, gave a series of retching coughs, then stood trembling, saliva drooling from her mouth.

The farmer turned to me, wide-eyed. 'You see, I had to get you out, didn't I? If I left her till tomorrow she'd be a goner.'

'You're right, Mr Kirby,' I replied. 'You couldn't leave her. There's something in her throat.'

We went into the pen and as the old man held the goat against the wall I tried to open her mouth. She didn't like it very much and as I pried her jaws apart she startled me with a loud, long-drawn, human-sounding cry. It wasn't a big mouth but I have a small hand and, as the sharp back teeth tried to nibble me, I poked a finger deep into the pharynx.

There was something there all right. I could just touch it but I couldn't get hold of it. Then the animal began to throw her head about and I had to come out; I stood there, saliva dripping from my hand, looking thoughtfully at Dorothy.

After a few moments I turned to the farmer. 'You know, this is a bit baffling. I can feel something in the back of her throat, but it's soft — like cloth. I'd been expecting to find a bit of twig, or something sharp sticking in there — it's funny what a goat will pick up when she's pottering around outside. But if it's cloth, what the heck is holding it there? Why hasn't she swallowed it down?'

'Aye, it's a rum 'un, isn't it?' The old man ran a gentle hand along the animal's back. 'Do you think she'll get rid of it herself? Maybe it'll just slip down?'

'No, I don't. It's stuck fast, God knows how, but it is. And I've got to get it out soon because she's beginning to blow up. Look there.' I pointed to the goat's left side, bulged by the tympanitic rumen, and as I did so, Dorothy began another paroxysm of coughs which seemed almost to tear her apart.

Mr Kirby looked at me with a mute appeal, but just at that moment I didn't see what I could do. Then I opened the door of the pen. 'I'm going to get my torch from the car. Maybe I can see something to explain this.'

The old man held the torch as I once more pulled the goat's mouth open and again heard the curious child-like wailing. It was when the animal was in full cry that I noticed something under the tongue — a thin, dark band.

'I can see what's holding the thing now,' I cried. 'It's hooked round the tongue with string or something.' Carefully I pushed my forefinger under the band and began to pull.

It wasn't string. It began to stretch as I pulled carefully at it . . . like elastic. Then it stopped stretching and I felt a real resistance . . . whatever was in the throat was beginning to move. I kept up a gentle traction and very slowly the mysterious obstruction came sliding up over the back of the tongue and into the mouth, and when it came within reach I let go the elastic, grabbed the sodden mass and hauled it forth. It seemed as if there was no end to it — a long snake of dripping material nearly two feet long — but at last I had it out on to the straw of the pen.

Mr Kirby seized it and held it up and as he unravelled the mass wonderingly he gave a sudden cry.

'God 'elp us, it's me summer drawers!'

'Your what?'

'Me summer drawers. Ah don't like them long johns when weather gets warmer and I allus change into these little short 'uns. Missus was havin' a clear-out afore the end of t'year and she didn't know whether to wash 'em or mek them into dusters. She washed them at t'finish and Dorothy must have got 'em off the line.' He held up the tattered shorts and regarded them ruefully. 'By gaw, they've seen better days, but I reckon Dorothy's fettled them this time.'

Then his body began to shake silently, a few low giggles escaped from him and finally he gave a great shout of laughter. It was an infectious laugh and I joined in as I watched him. He went on for quite a long time and when he had finished he was leaning weakly against the wire netting.

'Me poor awd drawers,' he gasped, then leaned over and patted the goat's head. 'But as long as you're all right, lass, I'm not worried.'

'Oh, she'll be O.K.' I pointed to her left flank. 'You can see her stomach's going down already.' As I spoke, Dorothy belched pleasurably and began to nose interestedly at her hay rack.

The farmer gazed at her fondly. 'Isn't that grand to see! She's ready for her grub again. And if she hadn't got her tongue round the elastic that lot would have gone right down and killed her.'

'I really don't think it would, you know,' I said. 'It's amazing what ruminants can carry around in their stomachs. I once found a bicycle tyre inside a cow when I was operating for something else. The tyre didn't seem to be bothering her in the least.'

'I see.' Mr Kirby rubbed his chin. 'So Dorothy might have wandered around with me drawers inside her for years.'

'It's possible. You'd never have known what became of them.'

'By gaw, that's right,' Mr Kirby said, and for a moment I thought he was going to start giggling again, but he mastered himself and seized my arm. 'But I don't know what I'm keeping you out here for, lad. You must come in and have a bit o' Christmas cake.'

Inside the tiny living room of the cottage I was ushered to the best chair by the fireside where two rough logs blazed and crackled.

'Bring cake out for Mr Herriot, mother,' the farmer cried as he rummaged in the pantry. He reappeared with a bottle of whisky at the same time as his wife bustled in carrying a cake thickly laid with icing and ornamented with coloured spangles, toboggans, reindeers.

Mr Kirby unscrewed the stopper. 'You know, mother, we're lucky to have such men as this to come out on a Christmas mornin' to help us.'

'Aye, we are that.' The old lady cut a thick slice of the cake and placed it on a plate by the side of an enormous wedge of Wensleydale cheese.

Her husband meanwhile was pouring my drink. Yorkshiremen are amateurs with whisky and there was something delightfully untutored in the way he was sloshing it into the glass as if it was lemonade; he would have filled it to the brim if I hadn't stopped him.

Drink in hand, cake on knee, I looked across at the farmer and his wife who were sitting in upright kitchen chairs watching me with quiet benevolence. The two faces had something in common — a kind of beauty. You would find faces like that only in the country; deeply wrinkled and weathered, clear-eyed, alight with a cheerful serenity.

I raised my glass. 'A happy Christmas to you both.'

The old couple nodded and replied smilingly. 'And the same to you, Mr Herriot.'

'Aye, and thanks again, lad,' said Mr

Kirby. 'We're right grateful to you for runnin' out here to save awd Dorothy. We've maybe mucked up your day for you but it would've mucked up ours if we'd lost the old lass, wouldn't it, mother?'

'Don't worry, you haven't spoiled anything for me,' I said. 'In fact you've made me realise again that it really is Christmas.' And as I looked around the little room with the decorations hanging from the low-beamed ceiling I could feel the emotions of last night surging slowly back, a warmth creeping through me that had nothing to do with the whisky.

I took a bite of the cake and followed it with a moist slice of cheese. When I had first come to Yorkshire I had been aghast when offered this unheard-of combination, but time had brought wisdom and I had discovered that the mixture when chewed boldly together was exquisite; and, strangely, I had also found that there was nothing more suitable for washing it finally over the tonsils than a draught of raw whisky.

'You don't mind t'wireless, Mr Herriot?' Mrs Kirby asked. 'We always like to have it on Christmas morning to hear t'old hymns but I'll turn it off if you like.'

'No, please leave it, it sounds grand.' I turned to look at the old radio with its chipped wooden veneer, the ornate scroll-work over the worn fabric; it must have been one of the earliest models and it gave off a tinny sound, but the singing of the church choir was none the less sweet . . . Hark the Herald Angels Sing — flooding the little room, mingling with the splutter of the logs and the soft voices of the old people.

They showed me a picture of their son, who was a policeman over in Houlton and their daughter who was married to a neighbouring farmer. They were bringing their grand-children up for Christmas dinner as they always did and Mrs Kirby opened a box and ran a hand over the long row of crackers. The choir started on Once in Royal David's City, I finished my whisky and put up only feeble resistance as the farmer plied the bottle again. Through the small window I could see the bright berries of a holly tree pushing through their covering of snow.

It was really a shame to have to leave here and it was sadly that I drained my glass for the second time and scooped up the last crumbs of cake and icing from my plate.

Mr Kirby came out with me and at the gate of the cottage he stopped and held out his hand.

'Thank ye lad, I'm right grateful,' he said. 'And all the very best to you.'

For a moment the rough dry palm rasped aginst mine, then I was in the car, starting the engine. I looked at my watch; it was still only half past nine but the first early sunshine was sparkling from a sky of palest blue.

Beyond the village the road climbed steeply then curved around the rim of the valley in a wide arc, and it was here that you came suddenly upon the whole great expanse of the Plain of York spread out almost at your feet. I always slowed down here and there was always something different to see, but today the vast chequerboard of fields and farms and woods stood out with a clarity I had never seen before. Maybe it was because this was a holiday and down there no factory chimney smoked, no lorries belched fumes, but the distance was magically foreshortened in the clear, frosty air and I felt I could reach out and touch the familiar landmarks far below.

I looked back at the enormous white billows and folds of the fells, crowding close, one upon another into the blue distance, every crevice uncannily defined, the highest summits glittering where the sun touched them. I could see the village with the Kirby's cottage at the end. I had found Christmas and peace and goodwill and everything back there.

Farmers? They were the salt of the earth.

# Chapter 21

Marmaduke Skelton was an object of interest to me long before our paths crossed. For one thing I hadn't thought people were ever called Marmaduke outside of books and for another he was a particularly well known member of the honourable profession of unqualified animal doctors.

Before the Veterinary Surgeons' Act of 1948 anybody who fancied his chance at it could dabble in the treatment of animal disease. Veterinary students could quite legally be sent out to cases while they were seeing practice, certain members of the lay public did a bit of veterinary work as a sideline while others did it as a full time job. These last were usually called 'quacks.'

The disparaging nature of the term was often unjust because, though some of them were a menace to the animal population, others were dedicated men who did their job with responsibility and humanity and after the Act were brought into the profession's fold as Veterinary Practitioners.

But long before all this there were all sorts and types among them. The one I knew best was Arthur Lumley, a charming little ex-plumber who ran a thriving small animal practice in Brawton, much to the chagrin of Mr Angus Grier MRCVS. Arthur used to drive around in a small van. He always wore a white coat and looked very clinical and efficient, and on the side of the van in foot-high letters which would have got a qualified man a severe dressing down from the Royal College was the legend, 'Arthur Lumley M.K.C., Canine and Feline Specialist.' The lack of 'letters' after their name was the one thing which differentiated these men from qualified vets in the eyes of the general public and I was interested to see that Arthur did have an academic attainment. However the degree of M.K.C. was unfamiliar to me and he was somewhat cagey when I asked him about it; I did find out eventually what it stood for; Member of the Kennel Club.

Marmaduke Skelton was a vastly different breed. I had been working long enough round the Scarburn district to become familiar with some of the local history and it seemed that when Mr and Mrs Skelton were producing a family in the early 1900's they must have thought their offspring were destined for great things; they named their four sons Marmaduke, Sebastian, Cornelius and, incredibly, Alonzo. The two middle brothers drove lorries for the Express Dairy and Alonzo was a small farmer; one of my vivid memories is the shock of surprise when I was filling up the forms after his tuberculin test and asked him for his first name. The exotic appellation pronounced in gruff Yorkshire was so incongruous that I thought he was pulling my leg; in fact I was going to make a light comment but something in his eye prompted me to leave it alone.

Marmaduke, or Duke as he was invariably called, was the colourful member of the family. I had heard a lot about him on my visits to the Scarburn farms; he was a 'right good hand' at calving, foaling and lambing, and 'as good as any vitnery' in the diagnosis and treatment of animals' ailments. He was also an expert castrator, docker and pig-killer. He made a nice living at his trade and in Ewan Ross he had the ideal professional opposition; a veterinary surgeon who worked only when he felt like it and who didn't bother to go to a case unless he was in the mood. Much as the farmers liked and in many cases revered Ewan, they were often forced to fall back on Duke's services. Ewan was in his fifties and unable to cope with the growing volume of testing in his Scarburn practice. I used to help him out with it and in consequence saw a lot of Ewan and his wife, Ginny.

If Duke had confined his activities to treating his patients I don't think Ewan would ever have spared him a thought; but Skelton liked to enliven his farm visits with sneers about the old Scotch vet who had never been much good and was definitely getting past it now. Maybe even that didn't get very far under Ewan's skin but at the mention of his rival's name his mouth would harden a little and a ruminative expression creep into the blue eyes.

And it wasn't easy to like Duke. There were the tales you heard about his savage brawls and about how he knocked his wife and children around when the mood was on him. I didn't find his appearance engaging either when I first saw him swaggering across Scarburn market place; a black bull of a man, a shaggy Heathcliffe with fierce, darting eyes and a hint of braggadocio in the bright red handkerchief tied round his neck.

But on this particular afternoon I wasn't thinking about Duke Skelton, in fact I wasn't thinking about anything much as I sprawled in a chair by the Ross's fireside. I had just finished one of Ginny's lunches; something with the unassuming name of fish pie but in truth a magical concoction in which the humble haddock was elevated to unimagined heights by the admixture of potatoes, tomatoes, eggs, macaroni and things only Ginny knew. Then the apple crumble and the chair close to the fire with the heat from the flames beating on my face.

The thoughts I had were slumberous ones; that this house and the people in it had come to have a magnetic attraction for me; that if this had been a big successful practice the phone would have been dinging and Ewan would be struggling into his coat as he chewed his last bite. And an unworthy thought as I glanced through the window at the white garden and the snow-burdened trees; that if I didn't hurry back to Darrowby, Siegfried might do double the work and finish the lot before I got home.

Playing with the soothing picture of the muffled figure of my boss battling round the farms I watched Ginny placing a coffee cup by her husband's elbow. Ewan smiled up into her face and just then the phone rang.

Like most vets I am bell-happy and I jumped, but Ewan didn't. He began quietly to sip his coffee as Ginny picked up the receiver and he didn't change expression when his wife came over and said, 'It's Tommy Thwaite. One of his cows has put its calf bed out.'

These dread tidings would have sent me leaping round the room but Ewan took a long swallow at his coffee before replying.

'Thank you, dear. Will you tell him I'll have a look at her shortly.'

He turned to me and began to tell me something funny which had happened to him that morning and when he had finished he went into his characteristic laugh — showing nothing apart from a vibration of the shoulders and a slight popping of the eyes. Then he relaxed in his chair and recommenced his leisurely sipping.

Though it wasn't my case my feet were itching. A bovine prolapsed uterus was not only an urgent condition but it held such grim promise of hard labour that I could never get it over quickly enough. Some were worse than others and I was always in a hurry to find out what was in store.

Ewan, however, appeared to be totally

incurious. In fact he closed his eyes and I thought for a moment he was settling down for a post prandial nap. But it was only a gesture of resignation at the wrecking of his afternoon's repose and he gave a final stretch and got up.

'Want to come with me, Jim?' he asked in his soft voice.

I hesitated for a moment then, callously abandoning Siegfried to his fate, I nodded eagerly and followed Ewan into the kitchen.

He sat down and pulled on a pair of thick woollen over-socks which Ginny had been warming by the stove, then he put on his wellingtons, a short overcoat, yellow gloves and a check cap. As he strolled along the narrow track which had been dug through the garden snow he looked extraordinarily youthful and debonnair.

He didn't go into his dispensary this time and I wondered what equipment he would use, thinking at the same time of Siegfried's words: 'Ewan has his own way of doing everything.'

At the farm Mr Thwaite trotted over to meet us. He was understandably agitated but there was something else; a nervous rubbing of the hands, an uneasy giggle as he watched my colleague opening the car boot.

'Mr Ross,' he blurted out at last, 'I don't want you to be upset, but I've summat to tell you.' He paused for a moment. 'Duke Skelton's in there with my cow.'

Ewan's expression did not flicker. 'Oh, right. Then you won't need me.' He closed the boot, opened the door and got back into the car.

'Hey, hey, I didn't mean you to go away!' Mr Thwaite ran round and cried through the glass. 'Duke just happened to be in t'village and he said he'd help me out.'

'Fine,' Ewan said, winding down the window, 'I don't mind in the least. I'm sure he'll do a good job for you.'

The farmer screwed up his face in misery. 'But you don't understand. He's been in there for about an hour and a half and he's no further forward. He's not doin' a bit o' good and he's about buggered an' all. I want you to take over, Mr Ross.'

'No, I'm sorry.' Ewan gave him a level stare. 'I couldn't possibly interfere. You know how it is, Tommy. He's begun the job — I've got to let him finish.' He started the engine.

'No, no, don't go!' shouted Mr Thwaite, beating the car roof with his hands. 'Duke's whacked, I tell ye. If you drive away now ah'm going to lose one of ma best cows. You've got to help me, Mr Ross!' He seemed on the verge of tears.

My colleague looked at him thoughtfully as the engine purred. Then he bent forward and turned off the ignition. 'All right, I'll tell you what — I'll go in there and see what he says. If he wants me to help, then I will.'

I followed him into the byre and as we paused just inside the door Duke Skelton looked up from his work. He had been standing head down, one hand resting on the rump of a massive cow, his mouth hanging open, his great barrell chest heaving. The thick hair over his shoulders and ribs was matted with blood from the huge everted uterus which dangled behind the animal. Blood and filth streaked his face and covered his arms and as he stared at us from under his shaggy brows he looked like something from the jungle.

'Well now, Mr Skelton,' Ewan murmured conversationally, 'How are you getting on?'

Duke gave him a quick malevolent glance. 'Ah'm doin' all right.' The words rumbled from deep down through his gaping lips.

Mr Thwaite stepped forward, smiling ingratiatingly. 'Come on, Duke, you've done your best. I think you should let Mr Ross give you a 'and now.'

'Well ah don't.' The big man's jaw jutted suddenly. 'If I was lookin' for help I wouldn't want 'IM.' He turned away and seized the uterus. Hoisting it in his arms he began to push at it with fierce concentration.

Mr Thwaite turned to us with an expression of despair and opened his mouth to lament again, but Ewan silenced him with a raised hand, pulled a milking stool from a corner and squatted down comfortably against a wall. Unhurriedly he produced his little pouch and, one-handed, began to make a cigarette; as he licked the paper, screwed up the end and applied a match he gazed with blank eyes at the sweating, struggling figure a few feet from him.

Duke had got the uterus about half way back. Grunting and gasping, legs straddled, he had worked the engorged mass inch by inch inside the vulva till he had just about enough cradled in his arms for one last push; and as he stood there taking a breather with the great muscles of his shoulders and arms rigid his immense strength was formidably displayed. But he wasn't as strong as that cow. No man is as strong as a cow and this cow was one of the biggest I had ever seen with a back like a table top and rolls of fat round her tail-head.

I had been in this position myself and I knew what was coming next. I didn't have to wait long. Duke took a long wheezing breath and made his assault, heaving desperately, pushing with arms and chest, and for a second or two he seemed to be winning as the mass disappeared steadily inside. Then the cow gave an almost casual strain and the whole thing welled out again till it hung down bumping against the animal's hocks.

As Duke almost collapsed against her pelvis in the same attitude as when we first came in I felt pity for the man. I found him uncharming but I felt for him. That could easily be me standing there; my jacket and shirt hanging on that nail, my strength ebbing, my sweat mingling with the blood. No man could do what he was trying to do. You could push back a calf bed with the aid of an epidural anaesthetic to stop the straining or you could sling the animal up to a beam with a block and tackle; you couldn't just stand there and do it from scratch as this chap was trying to do.

I was surprised Duke hadn't learned that with all his experience; but apparently it still hadn't dawned on him even now because he was going through all the motions of having another go. This time he got even further — a few more inches inside before the cow popped it out again. The animal appeared to have a sporting streak because there was something premeditated about the way she played her victim along before timing her thrust at the very last moment. Apart from that she seemed somewhat bored by the whole business; in fact with the possible exception of Ewan she was the calmest among us.

Duke was trying again. As he bent over wearily and picked up the gory organ I wondered how often he had done this since he arrived nearly two hours ago. He had guts, there was no doubt. But the end was near. There was a frantic urgency about his movements as though he knew himself it was his last throw and as he yet again neared his goal his grunts changed to an agonised whimpering, an almost tearful sound as though he were appealing to the recalcitrant mass, beseeching it to go away inside and stay away, just this once.

And when the inevitable happened and the poor fellow, panting and shaking, surveyed once more the ruin of his hopes I had the feeling that somebody had to do something.

Mr Thwaite did it. 'You've had enough, Duke,' he said. 'For God's sake come in the house and get cleaned up. Missus'll give you a bit o' dinner and while you're having it Mr Ross'll see what he can do.'

The big man, arms hanging limp by his sides, chest heaving, stared at the farmer for a few seconds then he turned abruptly and snatched his clothes from the wall.

'Aw right,' he said and began to walk slowly towards the door. He stopped opposite Ewan but didn't look at him. 'But ah'll tell you summat, Maister Thwaite. If ah can't put that calf bed back this awd bugger never will.'

Ewan drew on his cigarette and peered up at him impassively. He didn't follow him with his eyes as he left the byre but leaned back against the wall, puffed out a thin plume of smoke and watched it rise and disappear among the shadows in the roof.

Mr Thwaite was soon back. 'Now, Mr Ross,' he said a little breathlessly, 'I'm sorry about you havin' to wait but we can get on now. I expect you'll be needin' some fresh hot water and is there anything else you want?'

Ewan dropped his cigarette on the

cobbles and ground it with his foot. 'Yes, you can bring me a pound of sugar.'

'What's that?'

'A pound of sugar.'

'A pound of . . . right, right . . . I'll get it.'

In no time at all the farmer returned with an unopened paper bag. Ewan split the top with his finger, walked over to the cow and began to dust the sugar all over the uterus. Then he turned to Mr Thwaite again.

'And I'll want a pig stool, too. I expect you have one.'

'Oh aye, we have one, but what the hangment. . . ?'

Ewan cocked a gentle eye at him. 'Bring it in, then. It's time we got this job done.'

As the farmer disappeared at a stiff gallop I went over to my colleague. 'What's going on, Ewan? What the devil are you chucking that sugar about for?'

'Oh it draws the serum out of the uterus. You can't beat it when the thing's engorged like that.'

'It does?' I glanced unbelievingly at the

bloated organ. 'And aren't you going to give her an epidural . . . and some pituitrin . . . and a calcium injection?'

'Och no,' Ewan replied with his slow smile. 'I never bother about those things.'

I didn't get the chance to ask him what he wanted with the pig stool because just then Mr Thwaite trotted in with one under his arm.

Most farms used to have them. They were often called 'creels' and the sides of bacon were laid on them at pig-killing time. This was a typical specimen — like a long low table with four short legs and a slatted concave top. Ewan took hold of it and pushed it carefully under the cow just in front of the udder while I stared at it through narrowed eyes. I was getting out of my depth.

Ewan then walked unhurriedly out to his car and returned with a length of rope and two objects wrapped in the inevitable brown paper. As he draped the rope over the partition, pulled on a rubber parturition gown and began to open the parcels I realised I was once again watching Ewan setting out his stall.

From the first parcel he produced what looked like a beer tray but which I decided couldn't possibly be; but when he said, 'Here, hold this a minute, Jim,' and I read the emblazoned gold scroll, 'John Smith's Magnet Pale Ale' I had to change my mind. It was a beer tray.

He began to unfold the brown paper from the other object and my brain reeled a little as he fished out an empty whisky bottle and placed it on the tray. Standing there with my strange burden I felt like the stooge in a conjuring act and I wouldn't have been a bit surprised if my colleague had produced a live rabbit next.

But all he did was to fill the whisky bottle with some of the clean hot water from the bucket.

Next he looped the rope round the cow's horns, passed it round the body a couple of times then leaned back and pulled. Without protest the big animal collapsed gently on top of the milk stool and lay there with her rear end stuck high in the air.

'Right now, we can start,' Ewan murmured, and as I threw down my jacket and began to tear off my tie he turned to me in surprise.

'Here, here, what do you think you're doing?'

'Well I'm going to give you a hand, of course.'

One corner of his mouth twitched upwards. 'It's kind of you, Jim, but there's no need to get stripped off. This will only take a minute. I just want you and Mr Thwaite to keep the thing level for me.'

He gently hoisted the organ, which to my fevered imagination had shrunk visibly since the sugar, on to the beer tray and gave the farmer and me an end each to hold.

Then he pushed the uterus back.

He did literally only take a minute or not much more. Without effort, without breaking sweat or exerting visible pressure he returned that vast mass to where it belonged while the cow, unable to strain or do a thing about it, just lay there with an aggrieved expression on her face. Then he took his whisky bottle, passed it carefully into the vagina and disappeared up to arm's length where he began to move his shoulder vigorously.

'What the hell are you doing now?' I whispered agitatedly into his ear from my position at the end of the beer tray.

'I'm rotating each horn to get it back into place and pouring a little hot water from the bottle into the ends of the horns to make sure they're completely involuted.'

'Oh, I see.' I watched as he removed the bottle, soaped his arms in the bucket and began to take off his overall.

'But aren't you going to stitch it in?' I blurted out.

Ewan shook his head. 'No, Jim. If you put it back properly it never comes out again.'

He was drying his hands when the byre door opened and Duke Skelton slouched in. He was washed and dressed, with his red handkerchief knotted again round his neck and he glared fierce-eyed at the cow which, tidied up and unperturbed, looked now just like all the other cows in the row. His lips moved once or twice before he finally found his voice.

'Aye, it's all right for some people,' he snarled. 'Some people with their bloody fancy injections and instruments! It's bloody easy that way, isn't it!' Then he swung round and was gone.

As I heard his heavy boots clattering across the yard it struck me that his words were singularly inapt. What was there even remotely fancy about a pig stool, a pound of sugar, a whisky bottle and a beer tray?

# Chapter 22

'I work for cats.'

That was how Mrs Bond introduced herself on my first visit, gripping my hand firmly and thrusting out her jaw defiantly as though challenging me to make something of it. She was a big woman with a strong, high-cheekboned face and a commanding presence and I wouldn't have argued with her anyway, so I nodded gravely as though I fully understood and agreed, and allowed her to lead me into the house.

I saw at once what she meant. The big kitchen-living room had been completely given over to cats. There were cats on the sofas and chairs and spilling in cascades on to the floor, cats sitting in rows along the window sills and right in the middle of it all, little Mr Bond, pallid, wispy-moustached, in his shirt sleeves reading a newspaper.

It was a scene which was going to become very familiar. A lot of the cats were obviously uncastrated Toms because the atmosphere was vibrant with their distinctive smell — a fierce pungency which overwhelmed even the sickly wisps from the big sauce-pans of nameless cat food bubbling on the stove. And Mr Bond was always there, always in his shirt sleeves and reading his paper, a lonely little island in a sea of cats.

I had heard of the Bonds, of course. They were Londoners who for some obscure reason had picked on North Yorkshire for their retirement. People said they had a 'bit o' brass' and they had bought an old house on the outskirts of Darrowby where they kept themselves to themselves — and the cats. I had heard that Mrs Bond was in the habit of taking in strays and feeding them and giving them a home if they wanted it and this had predisposed me in her favour, because in my experience the unfortunate feline species seemed to be fair game for every kind of cruelty and neglect. They shot cats, threw things at them, starved them and set their dogs on them for fun. It was good to see somebody taking their side.

My patient on this first visit was no more than a big kitten, a terrified little blob of black and white crouching in a corner.

'He's one of the outside cats,' Mrs Bond boomed.

'Outside cats?'

'Yes. All these you see here are the inside cats. The others are the really wild ones who simply refuse to enter the house. I feed them of course but the only time they come indoors is when they are ill.'

'I see.'

'I've had frightful trouble catching this one. I'm worried about his eyes — there seemed to be a skin growing over them, and I do hope you can do something for him. His name, by the way, is Alfred.'

'Alfred? Ah yes, quite.' I advanced cautiously on the little half-grown animal and was greeted by a waving set of claws and a series of open-mouthed spittings. He was trapped in his corner or he would have been off with the speed of light.

Examining him was going to be a problem. I turned to Mrs Bond. 'Could you let me have a sheet of some kind? An old ironing sheet would do. I'm going to have to wrap him up.'

'Wrap him up?' Mrs Bond looked very doubtful but she disappeared into another room and returned with a tattered sheet of cotton which looked just right.

I cleared the table of an amazing variety of cat feeding dishes, cat books, cat medicines and spread out the sheet, then I approached my patient again. You can't be in a hurry in a situation like this and it took me perhaps five minutes of wheedling and 'Puss-pussing' while I brought my hand nearer and nearer. When I got as far as being able to stroke his cheek I made a quick grab at the scruff of his neck and finally bore Alfred, protesting bitterly and lashing out in all directions, over to the table. There, still holding tightly to his scruff, I laid him on the sheet and started the wrapping operation.

This is something which has to be done quite often with obstreperous felines and, although I say it, I am rather good at it. The idea is to make a neat, tight roll, leaving the relevant piece of cat exposed; it may be an injured paw, perhaps the tail, and in this case of course the head. I think it was the beginning of Mrs Bond's unquestioning faith in me when she saw me quickly enveloping that cat till all you could see of him was a small black and white head protruding from an immovable cocoon of cloth. He and I were now facing each other, more or less eyeball to eyeball, and Alfred couldn't do a thing about it.

As I say, I rather pride myself on this little expertise and even today my veterinary colleagues have been known to remark: 'Old Herriot may be limited in many respects but by God he can wrap a cat.'

As it turned out, there wasn't a skin growing over Alfred's eyes. There never is.

'He's got a paralysis of the third eyelid, Mrs Bond. Animals have this membrane which flicks across the eye to protect it. In this case it hasn't gone back, probably because the cat is in low condition — maybe had a touch of cat flu or something else which has weakened him. I'll give him an injection of vitamins and leave you some powder to put in his food if you could keep him in for a few days. I think he'll be all right in a week or two.'

The injection presented no problems with Alfred furious but helpless inside his sheet and I had come to the end of my first visit to Mrs Bond's.

It was the first of many. The lady and I established an immediate rapport which was strengthened by the fact that I was always prepared to spend time over her assorted charges; crawling on my stomach under piles of logs in the outhouses to reach the outside cats, coaxing them down from trees, stalking them endlessly through the shrubbery. But from my point of view it was rewarding in many ways.

For instance there was the diversity of names she had for her cats. True to her London upbringing she had named many of the Toms after the great Arsenal team of those days. There was Eddie Hapgood,

Cliff Bastin, Ted Drake, Wilf Copping, but she did slip up in one case because Alex James had kittens three times a year with unfailing regularity.

Then there was her way of calling them home. The first time I saw her at this was on a still summer evening. The two cats she wanted me to see were out in the garden somewhere and I walked with her to the back door where she halted, clasped her hands across her bosom, closed her eyes and gave tongue in a mellifluous contralto.

'Bates, Bates, Bates, Ba-hates.' She actually sang out the words in a reverent monotone except for a delightful little lilt on the 'Ba-hates.' Then once more she inflated her ample rib cage like an operatic prima donna and out it came again, delivered with the utmost feeling.

'Bates, Bates, Bates, Ba-hates.'

Anyway it worked, because Bates the cat came trotting from behind a clump of laurel. There remained the other patient and I watched Mrs Bond with interest.

She took up the same stance, breathed in, closed her eyes, composed her features into a sweet half-smile and started again.

'Seven-times-three, Seven-times-three, Seven-times-three-hee.' It was set to the same melody as Bates with the same dulcet rise and fall at the end. She didn't get the quick response this time, though, and had to go through the performance again and again, and as the notes lingered on the still evening air the effect was startlingly like a muezzin calling the faithful to prayer.

At length she was successful and a fat tortoiseshell slunk apologetically along the wall-side into the house.

'By the way, Mrs Bond,' I asked, making my voice casual. 'I didn't quite catch the name of that last cat.'

'Oh, Seven-times-three?' She smiled reminiscently. 'Yes, she is a dear. She's had three kittens seven times running, you see, so I thought it rather a good name for her, don't you?'

'Yes, yes, I do indeed. Splendid name, splendid.'

Another thing which warmed me towards Mrs Bond was her concern for my safety. I appreciated this because it is a rare trait among animal owners. I can think of the trainer after one of his racehorses had kicked me clean out of a loose box examining the animal anxiously to see if it had damaged its foot; the little old lady dwarfed by the bristling, teeth-bared Alsatian saying: 'You'll be gentle with him won't you and I hope you won't hurt him — he's very nervous'; the farmer, after an exhausting calving which I feel certain has knocked about two years off my life expectancy, grunting morosely: 'I doubt you've tired that cow out, young man.'

Mrs Bond was different. She used to meet me at the door with an enormous pair of gauntlets to protect my hands against scratches and it was in inexpressible relief to find that somebody cared. It became part of the pattern of my life; walking up the garden path among the innumerable slinking, wild-eyed little creatures which were the outside cats, the ceremonial acceptance of the gloves at the door, then the entry into the charged atmosphere of the kitchen with little Mr Bond and his newspaper just visible among the milling furry bodies of the inside cats. I was never able to ascertain Mr Bond's attitude to cats — come to think of it he hardly ever said anything — but I had the impression he could take them or leave them.

The gauntlets were a big help and at times they were a veritable godsend. As in the case of Boris. Boris was an enormous blue-black member of the outside cats and my bête noire in more senses than one. I always cherished a private conviction that he had escaped from a zoo; I had never seen a domestic cat with such sleek, writhing muscles, such dedicated ferocity. I'm sure there was a bit of puma in Boris somewhere.

It had been a sad day for the cat colony when he turned up. I have always found it difficult to dislike any animal; most of the ones which try to do us a mischief are activated by fear, but Boris was different; he was a malevolent bully and after his arrival the frequency of my visits increased because of his habit of regularly beating up his colleagues. I was forever stitching up tattered ears, dressing gnawed limbs.

We had one trial of strength fairly early. Mrs Bond wanted me to give him a worm dose and I had the little tablet all ready held in forceps. How I ever got hold of him I don't quite know, but I hustled him on to the table and did my wrapping act at lightning speed, swathing him in roll upon roll of stout material. Just for a few seconds I thought I had him as he stared up at me, his great brilliant eyes full of hate. But as I pushed my loaded forceps into his mouth he clamped his teeth viciously down on them and I could feel claws of amazing power tearing inside the sheet. It was all over in moments. A long leg shot out and ripped its way down my wrist, I let go my tight hold of the neck and in a flash Boris sank his teeth through the gauntlet into the ball of my thumb and was away. I was left standing there stupidly, holding the fragmented worm tablet in a bleeding hand and looking at the bunch of ribbons which had once been my wrapping sheet. From then on Boris loathed the very sight of me and the feeling was mutual.

But this was one of the few clouds in a serene sky. I continued to enjoy my visits there and life proceeded on a tranquil course except, perhaps, for some legpulling from my colleagues. They could never understand my willingness to spend so much time over a lot of cats. And of course this fitted in with the general attitude because Siegfried didn't believe in people keeping pets of any kind. He just couldn't understand their mentality and propounded his views to anybody who cared to listen. He himself, of course, kept five dogs and two cats. The dogs, all of them, travelled everywhere with him in the car and he fed dogs and cats every day with his own hands — wouldn't allow anybody else to do the job. In the evening all seven animals would pile themselves round his feet as he sat in his chair by the fire. To this day he is still as vehemently anti-pet as ever, though another generation of waving dogs' tails almost obscures him as he drives around and he also has several cats, a few tanks of tropical fish and a couple of snakes.

Tristan saw me in action at Mrs Bond's

on only one occasion. I was collecting some long forceps from the instrument cupboard when he came into the room.

'Anything interesting, Jim?' he asked.

'No, not really. I'm just off to see one of the Bond cats. It's got a bone stuck between its teeth.'

The young man eyed me ruminatively for a moment. 'Think I'll come with you. I haven't seen much small animal stuff lately.'

As we went down the garden at the cat establishment I felt a twinge of embarrassment. One of the things which had built up my happy relationship with Mrs Bond was my tender concern for her charges. Even with the wildest and the fiercest I exhibited only gentleness, patience and solicitude; it wasn't really an act, it came quite naturally to me. However, I couldn't help wondering what Tristan would think of my cat bedside manner.

Mrs Bond in the doorway had summed up the situation in a flash and had two pairs of gauntlets waiting. Tristan looked a little surprised as he received his pair but thanked the lady with typical charm. He looked still more surprised when he entered the kitchen, sniffed the rich atmosphere and surveyed the masses of furry creatures occupying almost every available inch of space.

'Mr Herriot, I'm afraid it's Boris who has the bone in his teeth,' Mrs Bond said.

'Boris!' My stomach lurched. 'How on earth are we going to catch him?'

'Oh I've been rather clever,' she replied. 'I've managed to entice him with some of his favourite food into a cat basket.'

Tristan put his hand on a big wicker cage on the table. 'In here, is he?' he asked casually. He slipped back the catch and opened the lid. For something like a third of a second the coiled creature within and Tristan regarded each other tensely, then a sleek black body exploded silently from the basket past the young man's left ear on to the top of a tall cupboard.

'Christ!' said Tristan. 'What the hell was that?'

'That,' I said, 'was Boris, and now

we've got to get hold of him again.' I climbed on to a chair, reached slowly on to the cupboard top and started 'Puss-puss-puss'ing in my most beguiling tone.

After about a minute Tristan appeared to think he had a better idea; he made a sudden leap and grabbed Boris's tail. But only briefly, because the big cat freed himself in an instant and set off on a whirlwind circuit of the room; along the tops of cupboards and dressers, across the curtains, careering round and round like a wall of death rider.

Tristan stationed himself at a strategic point and as Boris shot past he swiped at him with one of the gauntlets.

'Missed the bloody thing!' he shouted in chagrin. 'But here he comes again . . . take that, you black sod! Damn it, I can't nail him!'

The docile little inside cats, startled by the scattering of plates and tins and pans and by Tristan's cries and arm wavings, began to run around in their turn, knocking over whatever Boris had missed. The noise and confusion even got through to Mr Bond because just for a moment he raised his head and looked around him in mild surprise at the hurtling bodies before returning to his newspaper.

Tristan, flushed with the excitement of the chase had really begun to enjoy himself. I cringed inwardly as he shouted over to me happily.

'Send him on, Jim, I'll get the bugger next time round!'

We never did catch Boris. We just had to leave the piece of bone to work its own way out, so it wasn't a successful veterinary visit. But Tristan as we got back into the car smiled contentedly.

'That was great, Jim. I didn't realise you had such fun with your pussies.'

Mrs Bond on the other hand, when I next saw her, was rather tight-lipped over the whole thing.

'Mr Herriot,' she said, 'I hope you aren't going to bring that young man with you again.'

The publishers hope that this Large Print Book has brought you pleasurable reading. Each title is designed to make the text as easy to see as possible. If you wish a complete list of the Large Print Books we have published, ask at your local library or write directly to:

G. K. Hall & Co.
70 Lincoln St.
Boston, Mass. 02111